OBAMACARE

ON TRIAL

EINER ELHAUGE

Petrie Professor of Law at Harvard University
and Founding Director of the Petrie-Flom
Center in Health Law Policy

CONTENTS

PREFACE

Like most law professors, I did not take the constitutional challenge to Obamacare seriously at first. This is not because I favored its mandate to purchase health insurance. Indeed, I had publicly written in opposition to that mandate on policy grounds during the 2008 Obama campaign, when I was defending what was then Barack Obama's own opposition to the mandate favored by Hillary Clinton. But Supreme Court precedent made it implausible to think the mandate was unconstitutional.

As it became clearer that the threat was serious, I took a closer look and began to write about what I was finding in newspapers and magazines like The New York Times, The New Republic, and The Atlantic. It turned out that the constitutional challenge not only lacked any persuasive support in text, history, or precedent, but simply ignored the fact that the constitutional framers themselves had approved many purchase mandates, including mandates to buy health insurance itself! Instead, the challenge relied on a series of legal moves that had long been discredited in rigorous legal analysis, including: a formalistic reliance on linguistic labels rather than real functional effects; a distinction between action and inaction that was well-known to fail; and the argument that the existence of a political power could not be justifiable if one could imagine it might be abused in absurd ways.

This book collects the various essays I wrote about these weaknesses, many of which unfortunately were never raised in the briefs or oral arguments and thus were never addressed in the opinions of the Supreme Court justices. I have not modified any of these essays because I want to preserve the sense of real-time dynamic engagement with the arguments that were being made both in and outside the Court by supporters of the constitutional challenge. However, I have added Postscripts to some of the essays to reflect new or additional information that I was unable to include in the original essays.

Finally, I include at the end of this book excerpts from the opinion of Chief Justice Robert on the constitutionality of Obamacare's health insurance mandate, so you can judge for yourself whether you find it persuasive in light of my analysis.

IF HEALTH INSURANCE MANDATES ARE UNCONSTITUTIONAL, WHY DID THE FOUNDING FATHERS BACK THEM?

Einer Elhauge, The New Republic
(April 13, 2012)

In making the legal case against Obamacare's individual mandate, challengers have argued that the framers of our Constitution would certainly have found such a measure to be unconstitutional. Nevermind that nothing in the text or history of the Constitution's Commerce Clause indicates that Congress cannot mandate commercial purchases. The framers, challengers have claimed, thought a constitutional ban on purchase mandates was too "obvious" to mention. Their core basis for this claim is that purchase mandates are unprecedented, which they say would not be the case if it was understood this power existed.

But there's a major problem with this line of argument: It just isn't true. The founding fathers, it turns out, passed several mandates of their own. In 1790, the very first Congress—which incidentally included 20 framers—passed a law that included a mandate: namely, a requirement that ship owners buy medical insurance for their seamen. This law was then signed by another framer: President George Washington. That's right, the father of our country had no difficulty imposing a health insurance mandate.

That's not all. In 1792, a Congress with 17 framers passed another statute that required all able-bodied men to buy firearms. Yes, we used to have not only a right to bear arms, but a federal duty to buy them. Four framers voted against this bill, but the others did not, and it was also signed by Washington. Some tried to repeal this gun purchase mandate on the grounds it was too onerous, but only one framer voted to repeal it.

Six years later, in 1798, Congress addressed the problem that the employer mandate to buy medical insurance for seamen covered drugs and physician services but not hospital stays. And you know what this Congress, with five framers serving in it, did? It enacted a federal law requiring the seamen to buy hospital insurance for themselves. That's right, Congress enacted an *individual* mandate requiring the purchase of health insurance. And this act was signed by another founder, President John Adams.

Not only did most framers support these federal mandates to buy firearms and health insurance, but there is no evidence that any of the few framers who voted against these mandates ever objected on constitutional grounds. Presumably one would have done so if there was some unstated original understanding that such federal mandates were unconstitutional. Moreover, no one thought these past purchase mandates were problematic enough to challenge legally.

True, one could try to distinguish these other federal mandates from the Affordable Care Act mandate. One could argue that the laws for seamen and ship owners mandated purchases from people who were already engaged in some commerce. But that is no less true of everyone subject to the health-insurance mandate: Indeed, virtually all of us get some health care every five years, and the few exceptions could hardly justify invalidating *all* applications of the statute. One could also argue (as the challengers did) that activity in the health care market isn't enough to justify a purchase mandate in the separate health insurance market. But the early mandates required shippers and seamen to buy health insurance without showing they were active in any market for health insurance or even health care, which was far more rare back then.

Nor do any of these attempted distinctions explain away the mandate to buy guns, which was not limited to persons engaged in commerce. One might try the different distinction that the gun purchase mandate was adopted under the militia clause rather than the commerce clause. But that misses the point: This precedent (like the others) disproves the challengers' claim that the framers had some general unspoken understanding against purchase mandates.

In oral arguments before the court two weeks ago, the challengers also argued that the health insurance mandate was not "proper" in a way that allows it to be justified under the Necessary and Proper Clause. These precedents rebut that claim because they indicate that the framers thought not just purchase mandates but *medical insurance mandates* were perfectly proper indeed.

Postscript: Remarkably, this historical precedent for health insurance mandates was never briefed to the Supreme Court. Had it been, I think the case would have much easier, rather than the near-death experience it turned out to be. But this article triggered a firestorm of critiques on the conservative blogosphere, most notably *The Volokh Conspiracy*. The next two articles responded to these critiques.

A Response To Critics On The Founding Fathers And Health Insurance Mandates

Einer Elhauge, The New Republic
(April 19, 2012)

Last week, I wrote an article describing several purchase mandates adopted by the framers in early Congresses, including two medical insurance mandates imposed on shipowners and seamen. These examples rebut the claim by challengers to Obamacare that purchase mandates are wholly unprecedented in a way that allows us to infer they are unconstitutional, a claim on which they rely heavily because there is no text, history, or case law that affirmatively supports a ban on purchase mandates.

Not everyone agrees with me. Some comments to my article, here and elsewhere, have suggested that these early medical mandates are distinguishable from Obamacare because they reflect Congress' power to enact maritime law, not its power to regulate commerce. But the Constitution's list of congressional powers nowhere includes a maritime law clause. Early Supreme Court cases all held that the Commerce Clause was what gives Congress the power to enact maritime law. For example, in *The Daniel Ball*, a case decided in 1871, the Court stated that navigable waters form "a continued highway for commerce, both with other States and with foreign countries, and is thus brought under the direct control of Congress in the exercise of its commercial power. That power authorizes all appropriate legislation for the protection or advancement of either interstate or foreign commerce..." In *The Lottawanna*, the Court held that it was under this commerce clause power that Congress had enacted statutes that determined "the rights and duties of seamen" and "the limitations of the responsibility of shipowners." These early medical mandates were thus enacted under the very Commerce Clause at issue in the Obamacare case.

To be sure, later cases have held that Congress also has power to modify any judicial maritime common law, reasoning that this Congressional power is necessary and proper to regulate the judicial power to decide maritime cases. But these later cases do not alter the fact that the early federal maritime statutes were based on the Commerce Clause. Nor do these insurance mandates seem to fit within this additional power to alter maritime common law, which was about adjudicating disputes rather than imposing affirmative regulatory duties. Even if the mandates did fit, that would simply show that such mandates were "proper" under the necessary and proper clause.

Others—including the intellectual architect of the challenge to Obamacare, Randy Barnett—acknowledge that our early maritime statutes exercised the commerce power, but distinguish them on the ground that they were imposed on actors who were already in commerce. But this argument concedes that these precedents show that if one is engaged in commerce in one market, such as the shipping market or the seamen labor market, then Congress has the power to impose a mandate to purchase in a totally unrelated market—such as the medical insurance market. This concession conflicts with the argument of Obamacare's challengers, who claimed that widespread activity in the health *care* market did not permit a purchase mandate even in the highly related health *insurance* market. Indeed, this concession seems to make the whole action/inaction distinction collapse: If no relation between the markets is required, then commercial activity in any market would permit the Obamacare mandate. Because the Obamacare mandate applies only to those who have significant income that subjects them to income tax, it is necessarily limited to people who are already active in *some* commercial market. You cannot earn income without engaging in commerce. Thus, Obamacare satisfies the test that Barnett himself derives from these precedents.

Finally, some argue that the 1798 law requiring seamen to buy hospital insurance was a tax rather than a mandate. But the "duty" automatically deducted from seamen's wages under this law was not a general tax: The collected funds were segregated and had to be used to provide hospital coverage in the districts in which they were collected. This sort of mandatory payment into a segregated fund is indistinguishable functionally from a requirement to participate in a local hospital insurance pool. True, this statute did not require the seamen to provide proof of payment in order to receive hospital care. But the automatic nature of the deduction meant that proving one was a seaman was proof enough of payment. Nor does this argument distinguish Obamacare: Individuals currently do not have to provide any proof of payment in order to receive emergency hospital care, and part of the purpose of the Obamacare mandate was precisely to fund such emergency care.

In any event, the intrusion on free market choices is identical, whether we call the required payment a mandate or an earmarked tax.

Postscript: It turns out that, in this Article, I conceded more than I should have on the 1798 Act. Although the words of the statute did not state so explicitly, historical work by Professor Gautham Rao has shown that in fact seamen could get this hospital care only if they presented a certificate proving they had paid their duty, just like modern insurance requires presenting an insurance card showing you paid your premium.

A Further Response To Critics On The Founding Fathers And Insurance Mandates

Einer Elhauge, The New Republic
(April 21, 2012)

Since I wrote last week about the remarkable eighteenth-century precedents for a health insurance mandate, several supporters of the challenge to Obamacare have attempted to downplay the relevance of those early mandates for today's case. The latest is Professor Phillip Hamburger, who argues that those early statutes imposing health insurance mandates on private commercial shipowners and seamen didn't arise under the Commerce Clause; instead, he claims, they were justified under the power to provide for the Navy because such health mandates helped ensure "a large supply of healthy seamen" for the Navy to draft in the event of war.

This argument is certainly creative, but the connection between regulating private commercial activities and the Navy power is unconvincing. By that logic, one could equally say that the Obamacare mandate is justified because it helps ensure a large supply of healthy people to draft into the Army in the event of war. Nor does his Navy clause argument seem to fit the eighteenth-century statutes, which were replete with provisions requiring written labor contracts on key terms, regulating when wages had to be paid, and providing hospital care for disabled seamen even if they were no longer able to serve—none of which were relevant to ensuring a supply of healthy seamen to draft for war.

In any event, Hamburger's claim conflicts with Supreme Court case law, which as I have shown, does indeed hold that federal statutes regulating the duties of shipowners and seamen arose under the Commerce Clause. In contrast, I am unable to find any case holding that Congress' power to impose duties on private commercial shipowners and seamen arose under the Navy Clause.

Remember the context: The challengers are trying to infer a constitutional ban from purported silence because their theory lacks any affirmative support in the text, history, or case law. The constitutional text does not support the challengers' argument because, as conservative Judge Silberman held, 1780s dictionary definitions of "regulate" indicate that the plain meaning of the text giving Congress the power to "regulate commerce" does include a power to mandate purchases. Nor did any framer state that they thought the Constitution prohibited purchase mandates or any prior case so hold.

Bereft of such support, the challenge to Obamacare rests on the claim that the unprecedented nature of purchase mandates shows they were so wholly alien to the framers that they obviously would have wanted to ban them. Trying to infer a constitutional ban from a lack of precedent is dubious to begin with, since the Constitution has no anti-innovation clause, and the law presumes Congressional Acts are constitutional. But, if one is going to use that dubious method, one cannot exclude analogous precedents based on strained or technical distinctions.

Even if you do believe that these early mandates were justified under clauses other than the Commerce Clause, they demonstrate that the framers clearly thought purchase mandates were a "proper" means of executing constitutional powers. That's enough to show that the framers would hardly have been horrified at the notion of mandating purchases—and enough to validate the Obamacare mandate under the Necessary and Proper Clause.

Postscript: This article provoked the following remarkable admission by Randy Barnett, the intellectual architect of the challenge to Obamacare: "I never rested my claim that the individual insurance mandate was unconstitutional on the original meaning of the Constitution, and neither did the parties to the lawsuit."

Further research also revealed additional problems with Hamburger's claim that his reading was supported by the history showing that England and states had imposed similar seamen duties in part to aid the Navy. First, the history revealed that aiding the Navy was not the only purpose of these early statutes requiring seamen to buy health insurance: England and the states also cited the purpose of promoting commerce. Second, any historical purpose to aid the Navy is not in any event decisive because the United States has historically adopted many clearly commercial regulations – such as wartime wage and price controls – with the purpose of aiding the military.

THE BROCCOLI TEST

Einer Elhauge, The New York Times
(November 16, 2011)

The new mandate to buy health insurance has now reached the Supreme Court, which agreed on Monday to judge its constitutionality. The crux of the constitutional complaint against the mandate is that Congress's ability to regulate commerce has never been understood to give it the power to force Americans to buy insurance, or anything else.

But not only is there a precedent for this, there is also clear support for it in the Constitution. For decades, Americans have been subject to a mandate to buy a health insurance plan — Medicare. Check your paystub, and you will see where your contributions have been deducted, whether or not you wanted Medicare health insurance.

Many opponents dismiss this argument because Medicare (unlike the new mandate) requires the purchase of health insurance as a condition of entering into a voluntary commercial relationship, namely employment, which Congress can regulate under the commerce clause. Thus, they say, the Medicare requirement regulates a commercial activity, whereas the new mandate regulates inactivity. But is that a distinction of substance? After all, we don't have much choice but to get a job if we want to eat.

Even if you accept this distinction, it means that Congress can mandate the purchase of health insurance as long as it conditions that mandate on engagement in some commercial activity. So the challengers would have to admit that a statute saying that "anyone who has ever engaged in commercial activity must buy health insurance" would be constitutional. This is effectively the same as the mandate, because it is hard to believe that anyone in this nation has never bought or sold anything in his life.

Even if there are a few hardy folks who grow or make everything they need, their activity can still be regulated because it affects commerce. The Supreme Court held in *Wickard v. Filburn*, in 1942, that growing and consuming your own wheat can be regulated under the commerce clause because it reduces demand for wheat and thus affects commerce. Accordingly, a statute saying, "anyone who has engaged in any activity that affects commerce must buy health insurance" would clearly be constitutional, and cover everyone, just like the new mandate. In the end, the opponents' argument is merely about how the statute is phrased, rather than about its substance.

Opponents of the new mandate complain that if Congress can force us to buy health insurance, it can force us to buy anything. They frequently raise the specter that Congress might require us to buy broccoli in order to make us healthier. However, that fear would remain even if you accepted their constitutional argument, because their argument would allow Congress to force us to buy broccoli as long as it was careful to phrase the law to say that "anyone who has ever engaged in any activity affecting commerce must buy broccoli."

That certainly sounds like a stupid law. But our Constitution has no provision banning stupid laws. The protection against stupid laws that our Constitution provides is the political process, which allows us to toss out of office elected officials who enact them. This is better than having unelected judges decide such policy questions, because we cannot toss the judges out if we disagree with them.

Nor are all required purchases stupid. It is not stupid to require us to buy air bags for our cars and pensions for our retirements. Nor would it be stupid to require us to buy life and disability insurance to make sure we have provided for our children. Whether the law should is up to our political process, not judicial second-guessing.

But the argument that the commerce clause does not authorize the insurance mandate is beside the point. The mandate is clearly authorized by the "necessary and proper clause," which the Supreme Court has held gives Congress the power to pass any law that is "rationally related" to the execution of some constitutional power. For example, although the Constitution nowhere gives Congress the power to criminalize interfering with the mail, Congress can do so under the necessary and proper clause because it is rationally related to the constitutional power to establish post offices.

Everyone agrees that the commerce clause authorizes other provisions in the new health care reform act — those that require insurers to insure the sick and restrict premiums. But without the mandate, these other provisions would encourage the healthy to put off buying insurance until they got sick. With only the sick buying insurance, premiums would skyrocket and the market could fall apart entirely. In short, even if the mandate were not directly authorized under the commerce clause, it is authorized under the necessary and proper clause as rationally related to the constitutional exercise of the power to regulate premiums and prohibit rejecting the sick.

There are, of course, limits to what Congress can do under the commerce clause. If it tried to enact a law requiring Americans to eat broccoli, that would be likely to violate bodily integrity and the right to liberty. But the health insurance mandate does not require Americans to subject themselves to health care. It requires them only to buy insurance to cover the costs of any health care they get.

Postscript. This article provoked hundreds of comments on the NY Times website, many critiquing everything from my intelligence to my honor. But some comments raised more reasonable questions, which I addressed in the following article.

THE IRRELEVANCE OF THE BROCCOLI ARGUMENT AGAINST THE INSURANCE MANDATE

Einer Elhauge, The New England Journal of Medicine (December 21, 2011)

The parties who have brought legal challenges to the Affordable Care Act's (ACA's) individual mandate to obtain health insurance claim that the Constitution's Commerce Clause authorizes the regulation of only commercial activity, not inactivity, and thus gives Congress no power to force individuals to buy a product. They argue that if the Supreme Court were to hold otherwise, then Congress could force us all to buy anything, from General Motors cars to broccoli. This claim is a red herring, however, because Congress could force precisely the same purchases even if the Supreme Court were to accept their arguments.

Accepting the challengers' line between activity and inactivity would do nothing to curb Congress's feared power to force purchases, because Congress could easily sidestep that line by rephrasing the law to provide that if we have ever engaged in commercial activity, then we must buy insurance, broccoli, or anything else — just as Congress can and does mandate nondiscrimination by private firms, for instance, simply because those firms engage in commerce. Such a law would regulate activity, but because everyone buys things, it would have the same effect as a simple mandate. One might try to make this line more meaningful by adding a requirement that the obligation be germane to the commercial activity, but such requirements have proven fuzzy in the past — and, in this case, could easily be satisfied in a way that still creates a mandate by providing that anyone who has ever received health care from a paid provider must buy health insurance.

Nor are the challengers correct that Congress can regulate only commercial activity. The Supreme Court has held since 1942 that Congress has Commerce Clause power to limit our ability to grow wheat that we consume ourselves and do not sell, reasoning that it suffices that this noncommercial activity encourages a commercial inactivity that in turn affects commerce — because those who grow their own wheat are not buying wheat from others, which reduces commerce in wheat. If Congress can regulate a *non*commercial activity that causes commercial *in*activity that in turn affects commerce in this relatively minor way, then surely it can directly regulate a commercial inactivity that affects commerce in as major a way as the mandate would.

Some argue that the wheat case is outdated. However, the Supreme Court explicitly reaffirmed it in 2005, in a case holding that Congress had Commerce Clause power to ban the medicinal use of home-grown marijuana. The decision in that case held that Congress lacked Commerce Clause power only when the regulation was not "economic" in nature. The health insurance mandate is clearly economic — indeed, much more clearly so than the sustained marijuana ban.

Others argue that the Constitution's framers could not possibly have envisioned a congressional power to force purchases. However, in 1790, the first Congress, which was packed with framers, required all ship owners to provide medical insurance for seamen; in 1798, Congress also required seamen to buy hospital insurance for themselves. In 1792, Congress enacted a law mandating that all able-bodied citizens obtain a firearm. This history negates any claim that forcing the purchase of insurance or other products is unprecedented or contrary to any possible intention of the framers.

Indeed, we already live under a mandate to buy health insurance, because we have to pay contributions to the Medicare trust fund. Some argue that Medicare contributions are a tax, not a forced purchase. But an obligation to pay money has the same effect whether we call it a tax or not. Indeed, the new mandate actually provides that one has to either buy health insurance or pay a tax. The penalty is similar in nature to, but usually much smaller in monetary value than, the higher taxes we have to pay if we don't get a home mortgage and therefore cannot deduct any mortgage interest from our taxes.

The objectors respond that the new insurance mandate was not called a "tax." But why should mere phrasing trump substance? Both Medicare and the new mandate entail obligations to pay money for health insurance. That is what matters, not the labels chosen to describe this reality. Because the objectors' tax–nontax distinction turns only on phrasing, like their activity–inactivity distinction, it similarly fails to prevent the feared power to force purchases. Even without Commerce Clause authority, Congress could achieve precisely the same result with its taxing power by requiring us to pay a "tax" whose revenue will go to buy health insurance — or broccoli — for ourselves.

Some argue that Medicare differs from the mandate because Medicare forces us to buy health insurance from the government, rather than from private insurers. But any concern about Congress forcing us to buy broccoli would hardly seem lessened if it further limited our options by requiring us to buy that broccoli from government stores. Moreover, Medicare actually allows beneficiaries to get their benefits through private insurers. So this argument collapses to the claim that the government could force us to buy health insurance only if it also gives us the option of selecting government insurance. It's hard to see how this claim addresses any concern about limiting Congress's power to force purchases. Furthermore, this claim seems oddly inconsistent with conservatives' opposition to adding a public option to the mandate (which would be constitutionally required if this claim prevailed) and with recent conservative proposals to fully privatize Medicare (which would be constitutionally precluded).

None of this means there are no limits to Congress's power. It simply means that Congress can enact economic regulations that merely require us to pay money without exceeding its powers under the Commerce Clause. Congress remains subject to many other limits, including those imposed by the political process and all the other substantive constitutional provisions, such as free speech, equal protection, and personal liberty. For example, our right to liberty has been held to prevent violations of bodily integrity and would probably preclude any law requiring us to eat broccoli — but such issues are not raised by the mandate, which requires paying for health insurance but does not require us to undergo health care.

However one interprets the Commerce Clause, it clearly does not apply to the states and thus cannot impede state legislatures from requiring purchases. And although all 50 state legislatures have always had this power, none of them has ever forced us to buy broccoli or anything similar. This fact seems ample proof that the political process prevents such ridiculous laws from passing. Although the individual mandate's challengers may have a point in deploring the "nanny state," the solution is not to replace our democracy with "nanny judges" who tell us which laws we can pass.

Even if one did not want to recognize a Commerce Clause authority to force purchases, the mandate would remain constitutional under the Necessary and Proper Clause, because it is reasonably related to the ACA's provisions that prohibit discrimination against the sick, which are certainly permissible under the Commerce Clause. The reason is that without a mandate those provisions would encourage the healthy to put off buying insurance until they are sick, which could cause the health insurance market to collapse.

Some critics simply complain that the mandate is bad policy. I have to agree; indeed, like presidential candidate Barack Obama, I opposed the mandate. There are two ways to keep healthy people in the insurance pool: mandates and subsidies. Subsidies would have been not only more politically palatable, but also less regressive because they would rely on our normal tax system. Moreover, our current health care system is so inefficient that I would not have mandated the purchase of insurance without stronger reforms to increase its efficiency. I also hate broccoli. But there is a difference between the policies one disfavors and what the Constitution prohibits.

IT'S NOT ABOUT BROCCOLI!: THE FALSE CASE AGAINST HEALTH CARE

Einer Elhauge, The Atlantic (April 16, 2012)

The challengers of the health insurance mandate have focused on the Commerce Clause of the U.S. Constitution. As conservative Judge Silberman held, the text giving Congress the power to "regulate commerce" does seem to include a power to mandate purchases, given 1780s dictionary definitions of "regulate." The challengers argue that this plain meaning should nonetheless be resisted because otherwise the clause would lack any "limiting principle," and thus could be used to force us to buy GM cars, cell phones, burial insurance, or -- their favorite bugaboo -- broccoli.

But there is a limiting principle; it is the one the Supreme Court has actually articulated in its cases.

To be justified by the Commerce Clause, a federal law must (1) involve economic regulation (2) that addresses a national problem (3) that affects interstate commerce. That is a broad power, but it is not a limitless one. It does not, for example, authorize a federal law against committing violence against women or possessing a gun in a school zone because those are not economic regulations, as the Supreme Court has ruled.

So the problem is not that there is no limiting principle. It's that the challengers don't like the limiting principle that exists. They want the justices to read into the Commerce Clause a new limiting principle, one that bars laws mandating the purchase of any product. But however attractive that kind of new limiting principle might seem, it cannot be inserted into the Constitution by judicial fiat when it lacks support in the constitutional text, history, or precedent.

How does one address the terrible specter of a broccoli mandate? One response is that a broccoli mandate might not be valid under those existing limits, because there does not seem to be any national economic problem that has resulted from the failure of some of us to buy broccoli. But let us suppose one can concoct one by arguing that some hypothetical Congress might rationally think that the failure of some of us to eat broccoli makes us less healthy in a way that raises costs for others in our insurance pools. Let me further assume that, although such a hypothetical claim would be just plausible enough to meet the prevailing constitutional standard, a broccoli mandate would seem stupid to almost all of us. Does this ensnare us in a logical trap, forcing us to modify existing constitutional limits, to add a ban on purchase mandates? Not at all, for many reasons.

First, just because we may all agree that a certain type of law would seem stupid, does not mean the courts can insert a ban on such laws into the Constitution. The Constitution has no ban on stupid laws. The constitutional remedy for the enactment of a stupid law is voting out the stupid legislators who enacted it.

Second, if we all agree that a broccoli mandate seems stupid, then our political process will never impose it. Indeed, even the challengers admit that the states could adopt purchase mandates, and yet none of the 50 states has ever required us to buy broccoli, cell phones, cars, or anything else from the parade of horribles offered by the challengers.

Third, the challengers' argument would imply that the Commerce Clause must not give Congress any power to *ban* purchases of any product. After all, if Congress has such power, couldn't it enact outrageous laws *prohibiting* us from buying broccoli, GM cars, cell phones, or for that matter health insurance or even health care? The challengers' argument logically implies that because a power to prohibit could be used in these stupid ways, Congress's power to prohibit commerce also lacks a limiting principle. By that logic, judges should thus read new limits into Congress' power to prohibit commerce. But no one believes that would be proper constitutional law.

Fourth, suppose we imagine a future world where the political process has adopted one of the seemingly silly purchase mandates. If so, we might question our easy supposition that it was so stupid; the very fact of enactment would mean our democratic process us had concluded otherwise. If the Supreme Court imposes its judgment that such a law would be undesirable, despite the lack of any constitutional basis, it will simply be allowing its preferences to trump democratic preferences.

Fifth, like any constitutional power, the Commerce Clause is subject to other constitutional limits. In particular, the constitutional right of liberty has been interpreted in a way that bans laws violating our bodily integrity. This means that even if Congress could make me buy broccoli, it cannot make me eat it. All it can do is make me pay money, a classically commercial act. Likewise, the health insurance mandate does not require anyone to actually undergo medical treatment. It just makes us pay money.

Sixth, because purchase mandates are just an obligation to pay money, they are really no different from taxes. Indeed, the challengers conceded that Congress could have imposed a financially identical requirement if it had just used the language of taxes and tax credits. Thus, the challengers themselves have no limiting principle that precludes any of their parade of horribles. Under their theory, Congress could still impose the dreaded broccoli mandate by just calling it a tax that one can avoid if one buys broccoli.

Seventh, while the challengers' argument relies on imaginary mandates that no one is even thinking of proposing, the parade of horribles on the other side is very real. Adopting the challengers' new principle banning federal purchase mandates would throw into doubt a long list of existing federal laws that mandate commercial transactions. One federal mandate requires corporations to hire independent auditors. Another requires that unions buy bonds to insure against officer fraud. Federal statutes also mandate that hotels and restaurants commercially deal with minorities and disabled persons. Federal antitrust law sometimes requires monopolists to supply their rivals. The list is endless. Are all such federal mandates now going to be the subject of new constitutional challenges?

The more fundamental problem with the challengers' method is that it asks judges to impose new constitutional limits based on their own policy preferences about how to treat various hypotheticals. This method is even worse than directly asking judges to create new limits based on their policy preferences, because it never confronts the question of whether the health insurance mandate itself is so clearly a bad policy. Instead, it invites the justices to create a new limit based on their policy preferences about hypothetical *other* laws like the broccoli mandate--laws that Congress is likely to never enact--and then applies that limit to laws like the health insurance mandate that are far less silly as a policy matter.

Worse, this whole "limiting principle" methodology itself has no limiting principle. One could take *any* Congressional power that is defined by existing doctrine and argue that the doctrine would have no limiting principle if Congress could use it to adopt stupid laws. Judges would have to limit Congress' power to prohibit commerce, because it could be used to adopt stupid prohibitions like a ban on broccoli or health insurance. Judges would have to limit Congress' power to tax, because it could be used to tax us all 110% of our income and then throw us all in jail when that proved impossible to pay. Judges would have to limit Congress' power to declare war, since it could be used to declare war on Bermuda if Congress didn't like Bermuda shorts.

The deepest problem with the challengers' method is thus the parade of horrible *judicial* decisions that would be unleashed by allowing judges to create new constitutional limits unsupported by constitutional text, history, or precedent in order to preclude imaginary laws no one wants to enact. I share the challengers' aversion to the "nanny state," but it would be far worse to replace our democracy with "nanny judges" who tell us which laws we can adopt.

Postscript. Some have responded to one of my points – the one about states being able to impose precisely the same mandates – by arguing that the challenge to Obamacare was really about federalism – that is, about preserving independent state sovereignty. However, much of the challenger's argument clearly played on a concern that purchase mandates would infringe individual market liberty. Moreover, the federalism argument missed my point here: which was that the paucity of purchases mandates by state legislatures – which clearly had power to impose them – belied the claim that we could infer a lack of mandate power from a failure to exercise it, and also undermined the hysterical fear that if Congress had this power, it would begin mandating silly purchases right and left.

The federalism argument also had another major flaw that never got exposed before the Supreme Court and that I did not have room to address in this article. Namely, a federalism basis for a constitutional ban on Congress adopting a health insurance mandate cannot be squared with other well-established Supreme Court precedent, which clearly allows Congress to *prohibit* states from imposing health insurance mandates. This other precedent holds that federal ERISA law preempts any state law that requires certain insurance coverage if a firm is self-insured, which means states cannot mandate employer-provided health coverage. The combination of this precedent with any holding striking down the Obamacare mandate would have meant that the Court was interpreting the Constitution to mean that Congress cannot impose an insurance mandate but can prohibit the states from imposing insurance mandates. It would have been impossible to square that combination with any consistent federalism view of deferring to states. It could only be squared with a liberty claim of disfavoring mandates, a claim that cannot be found in the Constitution.

ECONOMISTS ARGUE OVER THE COST OF CARING FOR THE UNINSURED

Einer Elhauge, The Daily Beast (March 25, 2012)

Starting Monday, the Supreme Court will hear a grueling six hours of oral argument on the defining case of this term, and one of the most prominent in decades: whether the Affordable Care Act's requirement that everyone buy health insurance—known as the health-care mandate—is constitutional. The case has provoked an unprecedented 136 briefs for and against its constitutionality. Of all these, the two that everyone seems to be talking about are the opposing briefs by two groups of economists. When big-name economists collide, how can we sort out which are right?

The premise of the overall constitutional challenge is that the federal government cannot regulate "commercial inactivity." In other words, Congress may be able to regulate our commercial conduct, but it can't force us to engage in commerce, such as by making us buy ordinary products like broccoli or GM cars or, for that matter, health insurance. In fact, this premise is flawed. No constitutional text, history, or precedent has ever indicated that Congress could not regulate commercial inactivity. To the contrary, there are plenty of examples, going back to the very first Congress, where Congress has required us to engage in commercial activity— including making us buy health insurance.

But rather than debating this premise, the economists' briefs focus on the alternative defense that being uninsured actually involves commercial activity, not inactivity. The economists who support the mandate argue that none of us can control whether we will get sick and need health care next year. Thus, uninsured people generally cannot avoid being "commercially active" in health-care markets. They are, rather, a set of individuals who hope to be commercially inactive but predictably will actually be active. Indeed, 57 percent of the uninsured used medical services in 2007, and all but a few do so within five years.

Therefore, these economists argue, deciding to be uninsured is not "inactivity," but rather a commercial decision to self-insure the expected costs of unavoidable commercial activity. In other words—you're going to have to see the doctor eventually, so who pays? Because the uninsured often cannot afford the treatments they need, health-care providers will incur the resulting costs, either out of decency or legal duty, and then pass those costs on to taxpayers and the insured. Indeed, nearly two thirds of the costs of treating the uninsured are paid by others, with the total incurred by providers estimated by Congress to be $43 billion in 2008.

In contrast, if we decide we don't want to buy broccoli or a GM car next year, we are in full control of that decision. So, we can be inactive in ordinary markets in a way we cannot be for health care, where illness thrusts activity upon us.

So what about the economists who oppose the mandate?

They argue that the amount of cost-shifting caused by the uninsured is smaller than Congress's $43 billion figure. Many of their objections are economically powerful, but legally their effort falls flat because even they concede that the shifted costs are at least $12.8 billion, and the court has upheld federal laws based on far more trivial effects on interstate commerce. Moreover, in the end, the numbers don't matter: No one disputes that Congress may regulate commercial activity regardless of whether it imposes costs on others. So even if uninsured people cost us nothing, they are still "active" in the health-care markets, and the opposing brief does not really deny this (even though it quibbles about the precise extent to which that activity is unavoidable).

But, the mandate's opponents say, fixing the cost-shifting problem isn't really its central purpose. On the economics, they are right. Whatever the correct amount of cost-shifting, it is a small percentage of U.S. health-care spending. The central purpose was that, without the mandate, other provisions that prohibit discriminating against sick people by denying coverage or charging higher rates would encourage healthy people to put off buying insurance until they get sick. If this were to happen, premiums would go up and the insured pool would get sicker, until the market collapsed.

But their point fizzles legally. Under Supreme Court precedent, an effect on interstate commerce is enough to trigger regulation even if it is "indirect and fortuitous"—in other words, the act's main motive is legally irrelevant.

The antimandate economists' argument also suffers because it depends on the Supreme Court analyzing the case in a specific order. First, they argue, the court should consider the mandate on its own, and strike it down as primarily regulating inactivity. Then, they say, the court should strike down the law's other provisions—such as those prohibiting discrimination against the sick—on the ground that they cannot be severed from the mandate. (Other provisions are not "severable" from an invalid provision if it seems likely that Congress would not have wanted the other provisions in force without the invalid provision.)

But the court could easily reverse the order of analysis. It could first observe that it is undisputed that the law's nondiscrimination provisions are valid exercises of Commerce Clause power, and then note that it is also undisputed that those provisions could not function without a mandate. This produces the clear conclusion that, whether or not the mandate is authorized by the Commerce Clause, it is constitutional under the Necessary and Proper Clause as reasonably necessary to stop insurers from discriminating.

Finally, the mandate-opposing economists argue that the mandate amounts to a tax on the young and healthy, who will, given the nondiscrimination provisions, end up paying far more for health insurance than they can expect to receive in treatment. Again, this is sound on the economics, but it cuts the other way legally by showing that the mandate could alternatively be held constitutional under Congress's taxing power. The opponents argue this ground is unavailable because Congress failed to call the mandate a "tax," but this is a linguistic argument, not an economic one. It is also an argument that shows the opposition is not really about limiting the constitutional power of Congress, because they effectively concede that precisely the same mandate could still be imposed using different language.

In short, even if you buy the flawed premise that Congress cannot regulate commercial inactivity, the mandate-supporting economists persuasively show that being uninsured predictably involves unavoidable commercial activity, and costs taxpayers and others money. The mandate-opposing economists dispute the extent of those effects, but this is an issue where size really doesn't matter.

DON'T BLAME VERRILLI FOR SUPREME COURT HEALTH-CARE STUMBLE

Einer Elhauge, The Daily Beast
(March 28, 2012)

As the Supreme Court hears a final day of arguments over the health-care law, there is widespread agreement that in Tuesday's marquee matchup, U.S. Solicitor General Donald Verrilli—tasked with defending the law—had a rough go of it. But Verrilli is one of the most gifted advocates of his generation. So what happened?

To answer this it's helpful to consult one of the oldest battle treatises still in print. In "The Art of War," Sun Tzu defined a fundamental tenet of battle strategy: Never fight on the terrain that favors your enemy. The health-care law's challengers decided to frame this case as being about an unprecedented effort by the government to force the purchase of a product (in this case, health care). If that's what they thought the best framing was, you can be sure it was not the best framing for the government. And yet the government inexplicably offered no alternative framing in the months leading up to this week's showdown.

In fact, the challengers' claim is completely false. In 1790, the very first Congress (which included 20 framers of the Constitution, in case Justices Thomas and Scalia are counting), enacted a law requiring shipowners to buy medical insurance for seamen. The law was signed by another notable framer, President George Washington. Congress followed this with a 1792 law requiring all able-bodied citizens to buy a firearm, and a 1798 law requiring seamen to buy hospital insurance for themselves. Today there are a host of affirmative federal duties to buy things. For example, federal law requires corporations to hire independent auditors, and requires unions to buy insurance bonds in case their officers engage in fraud. The list goes on.

In all these cases (other than the firearms case), one could say the federal duty was imposed on persons who are already engaged in some commerce. But that is also true of everyone subject to the health-insurance mandate, because all of us buy or sell something. And yet in each case, Congress required people to enter into commerce in a different market than the one in which they voluntarily operate, which is precisely what the health-care law's challengers claim makes this mandate "unprecedented."

(Indeed, the challengers relied on a distinction between the markets for health care and health insurance that is far thinner than the one between the markets for, say, shipping and health insurance.)

It would have been much better had Verrilli raised these precedents—especially the ones involving the framers—when he was confronted with the claim that Congress has never required anyone to purchase anything before. But one can see why he might have chosen the more cautious route, since citing the precedents would have required him to squarely admit that, "Yes, Virginia (and Florida), there is a government power to make us buy broccoli."

Nevertheless, his failure to cite them left Justice Anthony Kennedy under the false premise that, as he put it, the mandate to buy insurance "changes the relationship of the Federal Government to the individual in the very fundamental way." That's just not true, and yet he relied on that premise to say that the government thus has "a heavy burden of justification" in defending the law.

Verrilli had a good alternative argument: Although the uninsured might seem like they don't participate in commerce, they are actually predictably active in the health-care market because we all get sick eventually, and when the uninsured end up needing medical care, others pay most of the cost. This argument is right on the economics, but it's dangerous to hang your hat on it, since saying that failing to buy insurance equals commercial activity isn't exactly intuitive for those without a PhD in economics.

Had the government more squarely attacked the challenger's framing of the case months ago, it would have been much clearer to everyone why this case is not at all about a fundamental change in the relationship of individual to government. Fighting on this more favorable terrain, the government could've also better exploited the fact that the law's opponents ultimately conceded that the mandate would be constitutional if Congress just called it a tax (or tax credit), or if it had been imposed by a state. It is hard to assert that "this mandate fundamentally alters the relationship of individual to government" and at the same time admit that "it would all be hunky dory if the mandate either used different language or was adopted by states."

In the end, it may not matter. Justice Kennedy and Chief Justice John Roberts ultimately expressed some sympathy with the Solicitor General's position that the uninsured were inevitably active in the health care market in a way that justified Congressional action under the Commerce Clause. But Verrilli's case would have been easier had the government read up on its Sun Tzu and not simply accepted the opponents' framing of the case.

THE ROBERTS-KAGAN COMPROMISE ON OBAMACARE?

Einer Elhauge, The National Law Journal (March 28, 2012)[1]

The oral arguments on the health insurance mandate did not go especially well for the government, in part because it mistakenly chose to accept the opponents' erroneous framing that it would be unprecedented for Congress to require individuals to purchase something. But even though it needlessly gave itself an uphill burden by accepting this mistaken framing, the comments of Chief Justice John Roberts Jr. and Justice Elena Kagan suggested a compromise that might still save the health insurance mandate.

---

[1] This Article is reprinted with permission from the March 28, 2012 edition of the National Law Journal © 2012 ALM media Properties, LLC. All rights reserved. Further duplication without permission is prohibited. For information, contact 877-257-3382 or reprints@alm.com or visit www.almreprints.com.

Rather than forthrightly arguing that in fact a lot of precedent indicated Congress could require individuals to purchase something, the government chose to rely solely on the alternative argument that the uninsured were as a class active in the health care market. The government had some strong evidence that most of the uninsured received health care within a year and almost all did within five years, and that when they did, two-thirds of the cost were borne by others when the uninsured were unable to pay for it. Thus, the government argued, those choosing to be uninsured were nonetheless, as a class, predictively active in health care markets in ways that cost the rest of us money.

The four liberal justices clearly seemed to buy this argument. Chief Justice Roberts and Justice Anthony Kennedy seemed somewhat sympathetic as well, notwithstanding their general skepticism about whether Congress could impose a duty to engage in commerce. The challengers to the mandate responded that each year many of the uninsured did not end up getting health care and an even smaller percentage ended up being unable to pay for it. Chief Justice Robert's response was "Yet we don't know who they are."

Here is where Justice Elena Kagan's comments suggested an intriguing possible compromise. She followed up Chief Justice Robert's remarks by noting that the case "might be different if you were…presenting a class of people whom you could say clearly would not be in the health care market." (For example, she had earlier observed that the case would be different if the opponents were representing a "a class of Christian Scientists" who were religiously opposed to accepting medical treatment and thus could convincingly show that they would not be active in the health care market.) The problem here, as she put it, was that "you're raising a facial challenge and we can't really know which, which of the many, many, people that this law addresses in fact will not participate in the health care market and in fact will not impose costs on all the rest of us."

This suggests a possible compromise that a majority of the Court might unite around. Namely, the Court could hold that: (1) this facial challenge to the application of the mandate to everyone fails because the challengers could not show which of the uninsured would not be active in health care markets, but (2) the mandate might be unconstitutional as applied to a more narrow class of persons who could prove they would never purchase health care.

This compromise could provide Justice Kagan's hypothetical class of Christian Scientists with a constitutional exemption from the mandate that they would otherwise lack. (Although the statute has a religious exemption, it is limited to religions that oppose any form of social insurance, including retirement benefits, and thus does not cover religions that solely object to medical treatment.) More broadly, this compromise could give the Court a way of sustaining the mandate while still finding a constitutional limit that could apply to any other group that could definitely prove they would not buy health care. This might include, for example, a group of libertarians willing to sign a "dying will" that commits to waive the right to be treated even in the case of emergency.

This sort of compromise could give both sides what they want most. It would give one side the practical right to require insurance for the vast bulk of people who cannot assure they will not end up getting health care. But it would give the other side affirmation that Congress cannot obligate persons to enter into a market that they can show they would otherwise avoid.

Postscript. Many have argued that Chief Justice Roberts ended up sustaining Obamacare because of institutional concerns about provoking a backlash against the Court for intervening into political matters. If that was his motivation, I think the sort of compromise outlined here would have served him better because it would have avoided that backlash while also minimizing the opposing political backlash he suffered at the hands of conservatives. The approach outlined here would instead have allowed him to fully validate the conservative claim that people should never be penalized for not participating in a market, while still sustaining Obamacare in general because very few uninsured could really prove they would not participate in health care markets. It thus would have allowed him to achieve the same institutional benefits, while making him less of a target for conservative critics. But all this matters only if his decision was motivated by those institutional factors. On a purely legal basis, he was right to sustain the entire mandate.

WHAT A NOBEL PRIZE-WINNING ECONOMIST CAN TEACH US ABOUT OBAMACARE

Kevin Caves & Einer Elhauge, The Atlantic (May 23 2012)

Ronald Coase won the Nobel Prize in Economics for showing that social costs are symmetrical. In The Problem of Social Cost, Coase invoked the example of a farmer whose crops are trampled by the neighboring rancher's cattle. Before Coase, it would have been common to view the rancher as the culprit responsible for imposing costs on the blameless farmer. Coase pointed out that no matter which way the legal rights were allocated, one was imposing costs on the other. If the law forces the rancher to keep his cattle fenced in, the farming imposes fence-building costs on the rancher. If the law gives the rancher the right to let his cattle roam free, then the farmer bears the social cost.

Coase's work was instrumental in establishing a new field of scholarship -- the economic analysis of the law, which has been highly influential in many legal areas. In light of this, it is surprising how little role the core Coasian insight had in the Supreme Court's recent oral argument about the Obamacare mandate. Much of the discussion seemed to take for granted that this mandate encroaches on individual liberty, depriving individuals of the "freedom" not to purchase health insurance.

But as Coase's analysis makes clear, framing the issue in terms of individual liberty is deeply misleading. When the uninsured get sick and go to the emergency room for care they cannot afford, someone has to pay the costs. If the law gives the uninsured the right not to buy health insurance, then the costs for their emergency care are imposed on the insured, whose payments must cover the hospital's costs. If the law instead requires the uninsured to buy health insurance, they become personally responsible for the cost of the care they receive.

In other words, the issue is not whether to have a mandate, but rather on whom the mandate should be imposed. If the Supreme Court strikes down

Obamacare, we will simply return to the old mandate, which was imposed on the insured rather than on the uninsured. It is not clear why that mandate would be constitutionally preferable to a mandate that everyone pay his or her own way. It surely does not involve any less of an infringement on liberty.

What is clear is that millions would not or could not obtain health insurance under the old mandate, which made health insurance less and less affordable to an ever-growing share of the population. This is why the Obamacare mandate was adopted. All the highfalutin' talk of the precious liberties at stake is an irrelevant, if highly effective, distraction.

Opponents asserted in oral argument that the Obamacare mandate went beyond this problem, by requiring more than catastrophic coverage, but this assertion seems to be mistaken. According to the Kaiser Family Foundation, the standard minimum "bronze" plans required under Obamacare would have an "estimated deductible of $4,375 for a single individual and double that for a family... a level of coverage that most would consider catastrophic."

Obamacare also explicitly allows anyone who is either under 30 or can show financial hardship to buy even skimpier plans that are undisputedly catastrophic. In short, the Obamacare mandate targets expensive treatments that would likely be unaffordable without insurance. The real debate is (or should be) over whether the mandate to pay for these treatments should be shifted from society at large to those who receive them.

A dose of Coase would go a long way towards clarifying the reality that the issue at stake is not individual liberty, but individual responsibility.

Postscript. I was very surprised that none of the justices seemed to address the point that the issue was not really whether to have a mandate, but on whom it would be imposed.

Another problem was that the challenger case boiled down to a mere claim about the *timing* for a mandate, rather than whether one could be imposed. The challengers conceded that Congress could mandate that people get insurance at the time when they actually get health care. Thus, their proposed constitutional limit turned solely on timing: they claimed that Congress cannot require us to get insurance in advance, but can after we get sick. But this conflicted with precedent that required deferring to Congress on mere matters of timing like this. Moreover, the notion that Congress might require us to get insurance after we get sick conflicts with the whole point of insurance, which is to protect against uncertain risks in advance. The challengers argued that Congress could create a spot market to buy insurance when the uninsured went to the emergency room. This is nonsense not only because such a spot market would be inadministrable, but also because the cost of that insurance would necessarily be at least the cost of care the person was about to get. And the very problem underlying the Act is that when the uninsured get sick, they often cannot afford that cost of care, so they are equally going to be unable to pay the cost of spot insurance. The challenger notion was like saying Congress could require us to buy fire insurance, but only after our houses have burned down.

EVEN THE MOST CONSERVATIVE SUPREME COURT JUSTICES HAVE ALREADY DECLARED MANDATES CONSTITUTIONAL

Emily Bass & Einer Elhauge, The New Republic (June 21, 2012)

Ever since the United States Supreme Court heard arguments about Obamacare's constitutionality in late March, speculation has been rife that the Justices will strike down the individual mandate. The predictions rest on a single assertion: That individuals have never before been required, under the authority of the Commerce Clause, to purchase a product or service from a private party. In other words, that there is no precedent for a "purchase mandate."

The assertion is inaccurate. There is not only clear precedent for such a mandate, but Justices of all political persuasions have embraced the precedent in principle. This includes nearly every member of the current Court. Only Justices Sotomayor and Kagan have never had the opportunity to weigh in on the issue.

So, what is the precedent?

In certain sectors, federal statutes have approved requiring employees to pay so-called "agency fees" to cover the cost of services received from a union acting as their collective bargaining agent, whether or not they wish to belong to the union. The 1956 *Hanson* case held that such a provision in the Railway Labor Act "is within the power of Congress under the Commerce Clause and does not violate either the First or the Fifth Amendments." Since then, the Supreme Court has repeatedly reaffirmed *Hanson*'s validity and the constitutionality of requiring that employees pay such agency fees. Indeed, as recently as 2009, the Court unanimously reaffirmed this principle in the *Locke* decision.

Strictly from the standpoint of their legal character, the health care and agency fee mandates are indistinguishable. In addition to both being "purchase mandates," they have the same justification. In the bargaining context, Justice

Scalia clearly and succinctly stated the rationale that is generally used to justify the imposition of agency fees in his opinion in the 1991 *Lehnert* case:

Where the state imposes upon the union a duty to deliver services, it may permit the union to demand reimbursement for them; or, looked at from the other end, where the state creates in the nonmembers a legal entitlement from the union, it may compel them to pay the cost. The "compelling state interest" that justifies this constitutional rule is not simply elimination of the inequity arising from the fact that some union activity redounds to the benefit of "free-riding" nonmembers ... What is distinctive ... about the "free riders" [here] ... is that, in some respects, they are free riders whom the law requires the union to carry ... Thus, the free ridership (if it were left to be that) would be not incidental, but calculated, not imposed by circumstances, but mandated by government decree.

In both the union and healthcare context, the disputed mandate to purchase services was justified to cover the costs of a prior mandate imposed on others to provide those services. In the case of agency fees, the prior mandate to provide services was imposed on unions: The government requires them to represent everyone in a bargaining unit, whether or not they have joined the union. The

Court held that this service mandate justified imposing the purchase mandate on those who are entitled to receive the services.

In the health care context, there are two relevant service mandates. The first was imposed about 25 years ago under a Reagan-era statute that requires virtually all hospitals to provide emergency services to anyone needing them, regardless of citizenship or ability to pay. The second service mandate is imposed by Obamacare itself, which requires insurance companies to "guarantee issue." This means insurers must sell a policy to any individual seeking to purchase one, without regard to "health status" or pre-existing conditions. It thus requires insurers to carry individuals and assume risks and costs that those insurers would not otherwise assume. Significantly, those challenging Obamacare's purchase mandate have conceded the constitutionality of each of these two service mandates—both the one imposed on the hospitals and the one on the insurers.

Given the union agency fees case law, these healthcare service mandates justify imposing an offsetting mandate to purchase insurance on all of us because we are all guaranteed those mandated healthcare services. Without such a purchase mandate, individuals could free ride on the service mandates by declining to buy insurance, knowing that they would still get emergency care they cannot afford and would still be able to buy insurance at low rates later when they get sick. Congress is thus entitled to impose a purchase mandate to make sure individuals cover: (1) the costs hospitals incur in providing emergency treatment, and (2) the costs that result from "guaranteed issue." Thus, the same free rider rationale that Justice Scalia cited in *Lehnert* to justify the agency fee purchase mandate applies equally to Obamacare's purchase mandate.

Altogether, this means that, if it is to be consistent, the Supreme Court has no choice but to uphold the constitutionality of Obamacare's purchase mandate. Not only are such purchase mandates not unprecedented, but a purchase mandate with a strikingly similar rationale has affirmatively been approved by all but two members of the current Court.

Update: At the same time that this opinion piece posted, the Supreme Court released its opinion in the *Knox* case, which indicated the justices might be aware of this potential inconsistency. The *Knox* case concerned the adequacy of a notice to opt out of a special dues assessment for political union activities, which the Court struck down, rather than a mandate to pay a union for its collective bargaining services. However, the opinion of the five conservative justices went out of its way to say that, while they "do not revisit today" the constitutionality of a mandate to pay for collective bargaining services, they now thought the free-rider rationale (which they had previously approved) was an "anomaly." This suggests that these justices may have anticipated the potential inconsistency between upholding the union fees mandate and striking down the health care mandate, and may be contemplating resolving this inconsistency by changing direction in the future on the underlying issue of agency fee.

Postscript. The *Knox* case left me thinking the Supreme Court would hold that the Obamacare mandate violated the Commerce Clause. But then I read Justice Scalia's dissent in the *Arizona* immigration law case, where he complained that "we should cease referring to it as a sovereign State." That led me to tweet the prediction, on the day before the decision was announced, that the Obamacare mandate must have been sustained. Had I been smarter, I would have realized that the combination of these clues meant I should have predicted it would be sustained under the Taxing Power but not the Commerce Clause power.

THE KILLER PRECEDENT FOR TODAY'S DECISION

Einer Elhauge, The New Republic (June 28, 2012)

Today's Supreme Court decision isn't just a victory for Obama and his health plan: It's a triumph of substance over formalism. The challengers' argument all along rested on a curious claim that linguistics should trump reality. They treated the mandate as a fundamental change in Congressional power, but conceded that precisely the same financial effects could have been imposed if the mandate had been called a tax. Likewise, for all their alarm about a broccoli mandate, their argument implied that Congress could impose it if it just called it a broccoli tax.

As a result, the challenger argument was never really about the scope of Congressional power, which would not have been changed even if they had won, but just about the words Congress must use to exercise it. It was just a one-off argument that would enable them to strike down Obamacare because, they argued, it used the wrong wording.

The Supreme Court, quite sensibly, rejected this position, holding that substance trumps linguistics. This was clearly correct. Tax precedents have long held that whether a levy is within Congress' taxing power depends not on labels, but on whether it has the same functional effect as a tax.

There are many such cases, but the killer precedent, which Chief Justice Roberts cited, was 1992's *New York v. United States*. That case involved a federal law mandating that states "shall" be responsible for disposing of their nuclear waste, enforced by what the statute said was a "penalty" of having to pay a higher surcharge on out-of-state nuclear waste shipments. The Court nonetheless held this was within the taxing power because the surcharge functioned as a tax—even though it didn't call itself a tax.

The Court's decision was not only based on clear precedent, it was also politically deft. By upholding Obamacare, but doing so as a tax rather than under the Commerce Clause, the Court probably minimized the effects of its decision on the upcoming Presidential election. The Republicans lose their claim that Obama acted unconstitutionally. They also lose the argument, which recent Romney comments suggest they were hoping to make, that Obama spent too much of his presidency securing a statute that ended up stricken. So the decision is certainly a net positive for Obama.

On the other hand, the Republicans will get to campaign on the fact that Obamacare was only upheld because it was a tax. This was a reality that the Democrats liked to minimize, but it will be hard to deny after the Supreme Court decision.

The upshot is that the decision improves our political process, rather than interferes with it. The campaign can focus on the reality: that Obamacare imposed a tax in order to try to secure health insurance for nearly everyone. People reasonably disagree about whether this goal was worth the tax. Now that disagreement can be resolved by our ultimate authority—which is not the Court, but the electorate.

Postscript. Although Roberts got the tax reasoning right, I think he got a lot else wrong in his opinion, as the next article reveals.

THE FATAL FLAW IN JOHN ROBERTS' ANALYSIS OF THE COMMERCE CLAUSE

Einer Elhauge, The New Republic (July 1, 2012)

Chief Justice Roberts was entirely correct in holding that the Affordable Care Act's individual mandate could be sustained as a tax. But in describing why that was the case, Roberts also revealed a fatal flaw in the section of his opinion that dealt with the Commerce Clause.

Roberts began his Commerce Clause analysis by stating: "Congress has never attempted to rely on *that power* to compel individuals *not engaged in commerce* to purchase an unwanted product." This clever phrasing allowed him to exclude from his claim the gun mandate (as not under "that power") and the prior mandates requiring shipowners and seamen to buy medical insurance (because they were "engaged in commerce"). Roberts then ruled that the Obamacare mandate went beyond the Commerce Clause, but nonetheless sustained it as within the taxing power.

But Roberts' tax argument actually undermines his argument about the inapplicability of the Commerce Clause. Roberts reasoned that Obamacare really imposes a mandate only on those subject to its tax penalty—which is limited to those who have thousands (probably tens of thousands) of dollars in earned income. What Roberts seems to have missed is that you cannot have earned income without engaging in commerce. (Gift income does not count as earned income subject to this tax).

Thus, Robert's own tax reasoning means that the Obamacare mandate applies only to those who *are* engaged in significant commerce; in other words, the health care mandate was never being applied to people who were "not engaged in commerce," the criterion so central to his Commerce Clause analysis. Since the insurance mandate regulates only those who are indeed engaged in significant commerce, it ought to fit easily within Roberts' own reading of the Commerce Clause.

But later in his opinion, Roberts does something sneaky. Although his textual reading of the

Commerce Clause and his claim about lack of precedent both turned on the claim that the mandate applied to someone engaged in no commerce at all, he later writes that the main problem was that "most of those regulated by the individual mandate are not currently engaged in any commercial activity *involving health care*."

But why did he introduce this new criterion? It's certainly not justified on the basis of precedent. The shipowners and seamen who in the 1790s were required to buy medical insurance were not engaged in any commercial activity involving health care; it was their engagement in shipping and seamen labor that was used to justify their health insurance mandate. Moreover, in the Obamacare case, the challengers implicitly conceded the constitutionality of Obamacare's employer mandate, which requires all sorts of employers who are not engaged in the health care market to buy health insurance for their employees.

In any case, it is easy to cite many other precedents that violate Roberts' claim that people engaged in one market cannot be forced to buy in another market. Federal law sometimes requires employees to pay fees for union representation even if they do not want that representation and are not engaged in the representation market. Federal law requires corporations to hire independent auditors even though the corporation was not in the audit market. Federal law requires unions to buy insurance bonds even though the union was not previously in the insurance market.

In short, Robert's analysis could be said to be reasonable in its claim that people engaged in no commerce could not be forced to buy something. But that claim does not apply to Obamacare. One senses that Roberts himself knew this; that would explain why, later in his opinion, he shifted his position, to claim that people who are engaged in commerce can only be forced to buy in the markets in which they are already engaged. But that proposition is not supported by text, history, precedent, or any other analysis that Roberts provided.

Postscript. I did not really have room in this article to get into the problems with Roberts' analysis of the Constitutional text, but it was beset with a parallel problem. He rejected the textual reading of conservative Judge Silberman that the power to "regulate" commerce included (under 1780s dictionaries) a power to "direct" commerce because that was only the second definition in those dictionaries. This tells us something about how malleable textualism is, when justices can pick and choose among the possible dictionary meanings. I would have thought that if dictionaries allow two possible readings, then the presumption of constitutionality, which Roberts himself stressed governs, means that one must adopt the reading that favors constitutionality.

But again the fatal flaw was that, even on Robert's reading, the commerce clause text excluded regulating only people who, as he put it, "are doing nothing." Given Robert's own equation of the mandate with the penalty that enforces it, the Obamacare mandate does not regulate people who are doing nothing. It regulates only those who are engaged in significant commerce. It thus easily fits within his reading of the text.

I also did not have room to address a technical exception to my claim that having the requisite taxable income necessarily requires engaging in Commerce. Namely, the income on prizes one receives without having applied for them, like the Nobel Peace Prize, are taxable even though one gave no consideration to get it. But it is hard to imagine there are many people who have no income from work or investments *and* receive enough prize income that this prize income alone brings them above the significant income thresholds necessary to be subject to the Obamacare mandate. It may even be that no single human fits this category, but certainly it cannot be more than a few. Thus, this technical exception could at most justify saying the Commerce Clause power did not apply to those few individuals. To hold it inapplicable as applied to others would be like saying that, if say *Wickard* came out the other way, then we could not have wheat production limits for farmers who do sell their wheat because a few farmers consume the wheat they produce.

Finally, another flaw in Robert's reasoning was that it relied on a present/future distinction that conflicted with past cases. Roberts concluded that the fact that the uninsured would predictably incur health care costs in the future could not justify imposing a mandate on them at present, before they did so. But this view conflicts with *Wickard* and *Raich*, which held that wheat and marijuana grown for home consumption could be regulated merely because it was *possible* that it could flow into the market at some future date. If that mere possibility of future commercial activity justified regulation, despite the absence of any evidence of how likely that possibility was, then the highly predictable future commercial activity of the uninsured should also justify regulation, especially given the evidence that 60% of the uninsured enter the health care market each year, and all but a few do so within five years.

ROBERTS' REAL LONG GAME?

Einer Elhauge, The Atlantic (July 20 2012)

Many are saying Chief Justice Robert's decision to sustain Obamacare was designed to preserve the long-term political capital of the Court. I think he simply made the decision he ultimately decided was right on the tax issue, which the precedent strongly supported. But to the extent a long-term political angle may have subconsciously motivated him, there is a large one that commentators have so far missed.

The unseen long game is that sustaining Obamacare as a tax helps preserve the Republicans' ability to adopt two items on their own political wish list: the Paul Ryan plan to privatize Medicare and George W. Bush's plan to privatize Social Security.

Consider the Ryan plan. It would convert Medicare into a voucher that seniors could use toward buying medical insurance from either Medicare or private insurers. The voucher amount would equal the cost of the second-cheapest plan, so if traditional Medicare is not one of the two cheapest plans, individuals would have to buy a private plan to avoid paying extra.

In short, under the Ryan plan, Medicare would become a mandate to make contributions into a Medicare trust that you would later draw from to buy yourself medical insurance, which could be from a private insurer, and might have to be so in order to avoid paying a penalty. This looks a lot like Obamacare's mandate to buy yourself medical insurance. There are two seeming differences, but neither is telling.

First, under the Ryan plan, the government would hold the mandatory contribution as a middleman. But it is hard to see why that should make a difference given that the Ryan plan requires the government to hold at least some of that money in trust for you, and you get to direct which insurer receives it. Nor does this feature distinguish Obamacare, under which government exchanges will also hold mandated contributions as a middleman for many people.

Second, under the Ryan plan, individuals can use their mandatory contributions to buy their insurance from a public provider. But that is the very public option that Republicans refused to allow in Obamacare, so it would seem odd to say that such a public option is constitutionally required. Nor does adding such a public option lessen any concern with mandating the purchase of insurance. No one argued that the feared "broccoli mandate" would have been fine if one had the option to buy that broccoli from a government store.

So, if Roberts had held that Obamacare was an unconstitutional mandate that could not be sustained under the taxing power, that would have created a serious risk that some later court would say the same about the Ryan plan. The same risk would have also imperiled any revival of the Bush plan, which effectively converts Social Security into an individual mandate to invest your Social Security contributions into a private retirement plan.

True, the Ryan and revived Bush plans could have tried to avoid this risk by using the word "tax" over and over to describe our mandatory contributions to their plans. But the one thing that is crystal clear from the tax power case-law is that it relies on function, not labels, to decide what counts as a tax.

So Roberts could have held Obamacare outside the taxing power only if he held that functionally it could not be treated as a tax. If so, then the Ryan or Bush plans are even less like a tax (no matter what label they bear) because if you don't make your required Medicare or Social Security contributions, you are subject to the full panoply of coercive IRS penalties, including criminal punishment. In contrast, Obamacare merely requires those with significant earned income to either obtain insurance or pay a small tax.

Maybe Roberts was not thinking about any of this. But a traditional judicial tool involves considering how any holding would affect a range of future possible cases. So this possibility strikes me as far more plausible than imaging he caved to political pressure, especially since Obamacare has (so far) not been that popular with the public anyway.

Whatever Roberts was thinking, one important effect of his decision is to preserve our nation's flexibility to try these sorts of mixed public-private approaches, rather than being limited to only statist solutions to our national problems.

CHIEF JUSTICE ROBERT'S OPINION

NATIONAL FEDERATION OF
INDEPENDENT BUSINESS V. SEBELIUS,
SECRETARY OF HEALTH AND HUMAN
SERVICES

132 S.Ct. 2566 (2012)

Chief Justice **ROBERTS**. [Because the Supreme
Court was divided, the structure of its opinions was
sufficiently confusing that some media outlets at
first reported it incorrectly. Four other justices
(Justices Scalia, Kennedy, Thomas, and Alito)
agreed with Roberts' conclusion (in Part III.A) that
the Commerce Clause did not authorize the
mandate, though they wrote a separate opinion on
that topic that used similar reasoning. But their

majority conclusion on the Commerce Clause did not affect the result because four other justices (Ginsburg, Breyer, Sotomayor, and Kagan) joined Roberts' opinion (in Part III.C) holding that the mandate was within the Taxing power. Because the mandate was constitutional as long as it was within at least one Congressional power, the majority holding that it was within the Taxing power sufficed to sustain the mandate in full.]....

III

The Government advances two theories for the proposition that Congress had constitutional authority to enact the individual mandate. First, the Government argues that Congress had the power to enact the mandate under the Commerce Clause. Under that theory, Congress may order individuals to buy health insurance because the failure to do so affects interstate commerce, and could undercut the Affordable Care Act's other reforms. Second, the Government argues that if the commerce power does not support the mandate, we should nonetheless uphold it as an exercise of Congress's power to tax. According to the Government, even if Congress lacks the power to direct individuals to buy insurance, the only effect of the individual mandate is to raise taxes on those who do not do so, and thus the law may be upheld as a tax.

A

The Government's first argument is that the individual mandate is a valid exercise of Congress's power under the Commerce Clause and the Necessary and Proper Clause. According to the Government, the health care market is characterized by a significant cost-shifting problem. Everyone will eventually need health care at a time and to an extent they cannot predict, but if they do not have insurance, they often will not be able to pay for it. Because state and federal laws nonetheless require hospitals to provide a certain degree of care to individuals without regard to their ability to pay, see, e.g., 42 U.S.C. § 1395dd; Fla. Stat. Ann. § 395.1041, hospitals end up receiving compensation for only a portion of the services they provide. To recoup the losses, hospitals pass on the cost to insurers through higher rates, and insurers, in turn, pass on the cost to policy holders in the form of higher premiums. Congress estimated that the cost of uncompensated care raises family health insurance premiums, on average, by over $1,000 per year. 42 U.S.C. § 18091(2)(F).

In the Affordable Care Act, Congress addressed the problem of those who cannot obtain insurance coverage because of preexisting conditions or other health issues. It did so through the Act's "guaranteed-issue" and "community-rating" provisions. These provisions together prohibit insurance companies from denying coverage to those with such conditions or charging unhealthy individuals higher premiums than healthy individuals. See §§ 300gg, 300gg–1, 300gg–3, 300gg–4.

The guaranteed-issue and community-rating reforms do not, however, address the issue of healthy individuals who choose not to purchase insurance to cover potential health care needs. In fact, the reforms sharply exacerbate that problem, by providing an incentive for individuals to delay purchasing health insurance until they become sick, relying on the promise of guaranteed and affordable coverage. The reforms also threaten to impose massive new costs on insurers, who are required to accept unhealthy individuals but prohibited from charging them rates necessary to pay for their coverage. This will lead insurers to significantly increase premiums on everyone. See Brief for America's Health Insurance Plans et al. as Amici Curiae in No. 11–393 etc. 8–9.

The individual mandate was Congress's solution to these problems. By requiring that individuals purchase health insurance, the mandate prevents cost-shifting by those who would otherwise go without it. In addition, the mandate forces into the insurance risk pool more healthy individuals, whose premiums on average will be higher than their health care expenses. This allows insurers to subsidize the costs of covering the unhealthy individuals the reforms require them to accept. The Government claims that Congress has power under the Commerce and Necessary and Proper Clauses to enact this solution.

1

The Government contends that the individual mandate is within Congress's power because the failure to purchase insurance "has a substantial and deleterious effect on interstate commerce" by creating the cost-shifting problem. Brief for United States 34. The path of our Commerce Clause decisions has not always run smooth, see United States v. Lopez, 514 U.S. 549, 552–559, 115 S.Ct. 1624, 131 L.Ed.2d 626 (1995), but it is now well established that Congress has broad authority under the Clause. We have recognized, for example, that "[t]he power of Congress over interstate commerce is not confined to the regulation of commerce among the states," but extends to activities that "have a substantial effect on interstate commerce." United States v. Darby, 312 U.S. 100, 118–119, 61 S.Ct. 451, 85 L.Ed. 609 (1941). Congress's power, moreover, is not limited to regulation of an activity that by itself substantially affects interstate commerce, but also extends to activities that do so only when aggregated with similar activities of others. See Wickard, 317 U.S., at 127–128, 63 S.Ct. 82.

Given its expansive scope, it is no surprise that Congress has employed the commerce power in a wide variety of ways to address the pressing needs of the time. But Congress has never attempted to rely on that power to compel individuals not engaged in commerce to purchase an unwanted product.FN3 Legislative novelty is not necessarily fatal; there is a first time for everything. But sometimes "the most telling indication of [a] severe constitutional problem ... is the lack of historical precedent" for Congress's action. Free Enterprise Fund v. Public Company Accounting Oversight Bd., 561 U.S. ——, ——, 130 S.Ct. 3138, 3159, 177 L.Ed.2d 706 (2010) (internal quotation marks omitted). At the very least, we should "pause to consider the implications of the Government's arguments" when confronted with such new conceptions of federal power. Lopez, supra, at 564, 115 S.Ct. 1624.

FN3. The examples of other congressional mandates cited by Justice GINSBURG, post, at 2627, n. 10 (opinion concurring in part, concurring in judgment in part, and dissenting in part), are not to the contrary. Each of those mandates—to report for jury duty, to register for the draft, to purchase firearms in anticipation of militia service, to exchange gold currency for paper currency, and to file a tax return—are based on constitutional provisions other than the Commerce Clause. See Art. I, § 8, cl. 9 (to "constitute Tribunals inferior to the supreme Court"); id., cl. 12 (to "raise and support Armies"); id., cl. 16 (to "provide for organizing, arming, and disciplining, the Militia"); id., cl. 5 (to "coin Money"); id., cl. 1 (to "lay and collect Taxes").

The Constitution grants Congress the power to "regulate Commerce." Art. I, § 8, cl. 3 (emphasis added). The power to regulate commerce presupposes the existence of commercial activity to be regulated. If the power to "regulate" something included the power to create it, many of the provisions in the Constitution would be superfluous. For example, the Constitution gives Congress the power to "coin Money," in addition to the power to "regulate the Value thereof." Id., cl. 5. And it gives Congress the power to "raise and support Armies" and to "provide and maintain a Navy," in addition to the power to "make Rules for the Government and Regulation of the land and naval Forces." Id., cls. 12–14. If the power to regulate the armed forces or the value of money included the power to bring the subject of the regulation into existence, the specific grant of such powers would have been unnecessary. The language of the Constitution reflects the natural understanding that the power to regulate assumes there is already something to be regulated. See Gibbons, 9 Wheat., at 188 ("[T]he enlightened patriots who framed our constitution, and the people who adopted it, must be understood to have employed words in their natural sense, and to have intended what they have said").FN4

FN4. Justice GINSBURG suggests that "at the time the Constitution was framed, to 'regulate' meant, among other things, to require action." Post, at 2621 (citing Seven–Sky v. Holder, 661 F.3d 1, 16 (C.A.D.C.2011); brackets and some internal quotation marks omitted). But to reach this conclusion, the case cited by Justice GINSBURG relied on a dictionary in which "[t]o order; to command" was the fifth-alternative definition of "to direct," which was itself the second-alternative definition of "to regulate." See Seven–Sky, supra, at 16 (citing S. Johnson, Dictionary of the English Language (4th ed. 1773) (reprinted 1978)). It is unlikely that the Framers had such an obscure meaning in mind when they used the word "regulate." Far more commonly, "[t]o regulate" meant "[t]o adjust by rule or method," which presupposes something to adjust. 2 Johnson, supra, at 1619; see also Gibbons, 9 Wheat., at 196 (defining the commerce power as the power "to prescribe the rule by which commerce is to be governed").

Our precedent also reflects this understanding. As expansive as our cases construing the scope of the commerce power have been, they all have one thing in common: They uniformly describe the power as reaching "activity." It is nearly impossible to avoid the word when quoting them. See, e.g., Lopez, supra, at 560, 115 S.Ct. 1624 ("Where economic activity substantially affects interstate commerce, legislation regulating that activity will be sustained"); Perez, 402 U.S., at 154, 91 S.Ct. 1357 ("Where the class of activities is regulated and that class is within the reach of federal power, the courts have no power to excise, as trivial, individual instances of the class" (emphasis in original; internal quotation marks omitted)); Wickard, supra, at 125, 63 S.Ct. 82 ("[E]ven if appellee's activity be local and though it may not be regarded as commerce, it may still, whatever its nature, be reached by Congress if it exerts a substantial economic effect on interstate commerce"); NLRB v. Jones & Laughlin Steel Corp., 301 U.S. 1, 37, 57 S.Ct. 615, 81 L.Ed. 893 (1937) ("Although activities may be intrastate in character when separately considered, if they have such a close and substantial relation to interstate commerce that their control is essential or appropriate to protect that commerce from burdens and obstructions, Congress cannot be denied the power to exercise that control"); see also post, at 2616, 2621 – 2623, 2623, 2625 (GINSBURG, J., concurring in part, concurring in judgment in part, and dissenting in part).

The individual mandate, however, does not regulate existing commercial activity. It instead compels individuals to become active in commerce by purchasing a product, on the ground that their failure to do so affects interstate commerce. Construing the Commerce Clause to permit Congress to regulate individuals precisely because they are doing nothing would open a new and potentially vast domain to congressional authority. Every day individuals do not do an infinite number of things. In some cases they decide not to do something; in others they simply fail to do it. Allowing Congress to justify federal regulation by pointing to the effect of inaction on commerce would bring countless decisions an individual could potentially make within the scope of federal regulation, and—under the Government's theory— empower Congress to make those decisions for him.

Applying the Government's logic to the familiar case of Wickard v. Filburn shows how far that logic would carry us from the notion of a government of limited powers. In Wickard, the Court famously upheld a federal penalty imposed on a farmer for growing wheat for consumption on his own farm. 317 U.S., at 114–115, 128–129, 63 S.Ct. 82. That amount of wheat caused the farmer to exceed his quota under a program designed to support the price of wheat by limiting supply. The Court rejected the farmer's argument that growing wheat for home consumption was beyond the reach of the commerce power. It did so on the ground that the farmer's decision to grow wheat for his own use allowed him to avoid purchasing wheat in the market. That decision, when considered in the aggregate along with similar decisions of others, would have had a substantial effect on the interstate market for wheat. Id., at 127–129, 63 S.Ct. 82.

Wickard has long been regarded as "perhaps the most far reaching example of Commerce Clause authority over intrastate activity," Lopez, 514 U.S., at 560, 115 S.Ct. 1624, but the Government's theory in this case would go much further. Under Wickard it is within Congress's power to regulate the market for wheat by supporting its price. But price can be supported by increasing demand as well as by decreasing supply. The aggregated decisions of some consumers not to purchase wheat have a substantial effect on the price of wheat, just as decisions not to purchase health insurance have on the price of insurance. Congress can therefore command that those not buying wheat do so, just as it argues here that it may command that those not buying health insurance do so. The farmer in Wickard was at least actively engaged in the production of wheat, and the Government could regulate that activity because of its effect on commerce. The Government's theory here would effectively override that limitation, by establishing that individuals may be regulated under the Commerce Clause whenever enough of them are not doing something the Government would have them do.

Indeed, the Government's logic would justify a mandatory purchase to solve almost any problem. See Seven–Sky, 661 F.3d, at 14–15 (noting the Government's inability to "identify any mandate to purchase a product or service in interstate commerce that would be unconstitutional" under its theory of the commerce power). To consider a different example in the health care market, many Americans do not eat a balanced diet. That group makes up a larger percentage of the total population than those without health insurance. See, e.g., Dept. of Agriculture and Dept. of Health and Human Services, Dietary Guidelines for Americans 1 (2010). The failure of that group to have a healthy diet increases health care costs, to a greater extent than the failure of the uninsured to purchase insurance. See, e.g., Finkelstein, Trogdon, Cohen, & Dietz, Annual Medical Spending Attributable to Obesity: Payer– and Service–Specific Estimates, 28 Health Affairs w822 (2009) (detailing the "undeniable link between rising rates of obesity and rising medical spending," and estimating that "the annual medical burden of obesity has risen to almost 10 percent of all medical spending and could amount to $147 billion per year in 2008"). Those increased costs are borne in part by other Americans who must pay more, just as the uninsured shift costs to the insured. See Center for Applied Ethics, Voluntary Health Risks: Who Should Pay?, 6 Issues in Ethics 6 (1993) (noting "overwhelming evidence that individuals with unhealthy habits pay only a fraction of the costs associated with their behaviors; most of the expense is borne by the rest of society in the form of higher insurance premiums, government expenditures for health care, and disability benefits"). Congress addressed the insurance problem by ordering everyone to buy insurance. Under the

Government's theory, Congress could address the diet problem by ordering everyone to buy vegetables. See Dietary Guidelines, supra, at 19 ("Improved nutrition, appropriate eating behaviors, and increased physical activity have tremendous potential to ... reduce health care costs").

People, for reasons of their own, often fail to do things that would be good for them or good for society. Those failures—joined with the similar failures of others—can readily have a substantial effect on interstate commerce. Under the Government's logic, that authorizes Congress to use its commerce power to compel citizens to act as the Government would have them act.

That is not the country the Framers of our Constitution envisioned. James Madison explained that the Commerce Clause was "an addition which few oppose and from which no apprehensions are entertained." The Federalist No. 45, at 293. While Congress's authority under the Commerce Clause has of course expanded with the growth of the national economy, our cases have "always recognized that the power to regulate commerce, though broad indeed, has limits." Maryland v. Wirtz, 392 U.S. 183, 196, 88 S.Ct. 2017, 20 L.Ed.2d 1020 (1968). The Government's theory would erode those limits, permitting Congress to reach beyond the natural extent of its authority, "everywhere extending the sphere of its activity and drawing all power into its impetuous vortex." The Federalist No. 48, at 309 (J. Madison). Congress already enjoys vast power to regulate much of what we do. Accepting the Government's theory would give Congress the same license to regulate what we do not do, fundamentally changing the relation between the citizen and the Federal Government.FN6

> FN6. In an attempt to recast the individual mandate as a regulation of commercial activity, Justice GINSBURG suggests that "[a]n individual who opts not to purchase insurance from a private insurer can be seen as actively selecting another form of insurance: self-insurance." Post, at 2622. But "self-insurance" is, in this context, nothing more than a description of the failure to purchase insurance. Individuals are no more "activ[e] in the self-insurance market" when they fail to purchase insurance, ibid., than they are active in the "rest" market when doing nothing.

To an economist, perhaps, there is no difference between activity and inactivity; both have measurable economic effects on commerce. But the distinction between doing something and doing nothing would not have been lost on the Framers, who were "practical statesmen," not metaphysical philosophers. Industrial Union Dept., AFL–CIO v. American Petroleum Institute, 448 U.S. 607, 673, 100 S.Ct. 2844, 65 L.Ed.2d 1010 (1980) (Rehnquist, J., concurring in judgment). As we have explained, "the framers of the Constitution were not mere visionaries, toying with speculations or theories, but practical men, dealing with the facts of political life as they understood them, putting into form the government they were creating, and prescribing in language clear and intelligible the powers that government was to take." South Carolina v. United States, 199 U.S. 437, 449, 26 S.Ct. 110, 50 L.Ed. 261 (1905). The Framers gave Congress the power to regulate commerce, not to compel it, and for over 200 years both our decisions and Congress's actions have reflected this understanding. There is no reason to depart from that understanding now.

The Government sees things differently. It argues that because sickness and injury are unpredictable but unavoidable, "the uninsured as a class are active in the market for health care, which they regularly seek and obtain." Brief for United States 50. The individual mandate "merely regulates how individuals finance and pay for that active participation—requiring that they do so through insurance, rather than through attempted self-insurance with the back-stop of shifting costs to others." Ibid.

The Government repeats the phrase "active in the market for health care" throughout its brief, see id., at 7, 18, 34, 50, but that concept has no constitutional significance. An individual who bought a car two years ago and may buy another in the future is not "active in the car market" in any pertinent sense. The phrase "active in the market" cannot obscure the fact that most of those regulated by the individual mandate are not currently engaged in any commercial activity involving health care, and that fact is fatal to the Government's effort to "regulate the uninsured as a class." Id., at 42. Our precedents recognize Congress's power to regulate "class [es] of activities," Gonzales v. Raich, 545 U.S. 1, 17, 125 S.Ct. 2195, 162 L.Ed.2d 1 (2005) (emphasis added), not classes of individuals, apart from any activity in which they are engaged, see, e.g., Perez, 402 U.S., at 153, 91 S.Ct. 1357 ("Petitioner is clearly a member of the class which engages in 'extortionate credit transactions' ..." (emphasis deleted)).

The individual mandate's regulation of the uninsured as a class is, in fact, particularly divorced from any link to existing commercial activity. The mandate primarily affects healthy, often young adults who are less likely to need significant health care and have other priorities for spending their money. It is precisely because these individuals, as an actuarial class, incur relatively low health care costs that the mandate helps counter the effect of forcing insurance companies to cover others who impose greater costs than their premiums are allowed to reflect. See 42 U.S.C. § 18091(2)(I) (recognizing that the mandate would "broaden the health insurance risk pool to include healthy individuals, which will lower health insurance premiums"). If the individual mandate is targeted at a class, it is a class whose commercial inactivity rather than activity is its defining feature.

The Government, however, claims that this does not matter. The Government regards it as sufficient to trigger Congress's authority that almost all those who are uninsured will, at some unknown point in the future, engage in a health care transaction. Asserting that "[t]here is no temporal limitation in the Commerce Clause," the Government argues that because "[e]veryone subject to this regulation is in or will be in the health care market," they can be "regulated in advance." Tr. of Oral Arg. 109 (Mar. 27, 2012).

The proposition that Congress may dictate the conduct of an individual today because of prophesied future activity finds no support in our precedent. We have said that Congress can anticipate the effects on commerce of an economic activity. See, e.g., Consolidated Edison Co. v. NLRB, 305 U.S. 197, 59 S.Ct. 206, 83 L.Ed. 126

(1938) (regulating the labor practices of utility companies); Heart of Atlanta Motel, Inc. v. United States, 379 U.S. 241, 85 S.Ct. 348, 13 L.Ed.2d 258 (1964) (prohibiting discrimination by hotel operators); Katzenbach v. McClung, 379 U.S. 294, 85 S.Ct. 377, 13 L.Ed.2d 290 (1964) (prohibiting discrimination by restaurant owners). But we have never permitted Congress to anticipate that activity itself in order to regulate individuals not currently engaged in commerce. Each one of our cases, including those cited by Justice GINSBURG, post, at 2619 – 2620, involved preexisting economic activity. See, e.g., Wickard, 317 U.S., at 127–129, 63 S.Ct. 82 (producing wheat); Raich, supra, at 25, 125 S.Ct. 2195 (growing marijuana).

Everyone will likely participate in the markets for food, clothing, transportation, shelter, or energy; that does not authorize Congress to direct them to purchase particular products in those or other markets today. The Commerce Clause is not a general license to regulate an individual from cradle to grave, simply because he will predictably engage in particular transactions. Any police power to regulate individuals as such, as opposed to their activities, remains vested in the States.

The Government argues that the individual mandate can be sustained as a sort of exception to this rule, because health insurance is a unique product. According to the Government, upholding the individual mandate would not justify mandatory purchases of items such as cars or broccoli because, as the Government puts it, "[h]ealth insurance is not purchased for its own sake like a car or broccoli; it is a means of financing health-care consumption and covering universal risks." Reply Brief for United States 19. But cars and broccoli are no more purchased for their "own sake" than health insurance. They are purchased to cover the need for transportation and food.

The Government says that health insurance and health care financing are "inherently integrated." Brief for United States 41. But that does not mean the compelled purchase of the first is properly regarded as a regulation of the second. No matter how "inherently integrated" health insurance and health care consumption may be, they are not the same thing: They involve different transactions, entered into at different times, with different providers. And for most of those targeted by the mandate, significant health care needs will be years, or even decades, away. The proximity and degree of connection between the mandate and the subsequent commercial activity is too lacking to justify an exception of the sort urged by the Government. The individual mandate forces individuals into commerce precisely because they elected to refrain from commercial activity. Such a law cannot be sustained under a clause authorizing Congress to "regulate Commerce."

2

The Government next contends that Congress has the power under the Necessary and Proper Clause to enact the individual mandate because the mandate is an "integral part of a comprehensive scheme of economic regulation"—the guaranteed-issue and community-rating insurance reforms. Brief for United States 24. Under this argument, it is not necessary to consider the effect that an individual's inactivity may have on interstate commerce; it is enough that Congress regulate commercial activity in a way that requires regulation of inactivity to be effective.

The power to "make all Laws which shall be necessary and proper for carrying into Execution" the powers enumerated in the Constitution, Art. I, § 8, cl. 18, vests Congress with authority to enact provisions "incidental to the [enumerated] power, and conducive to its beneficial exercise," McCulloch, 4 Wheat., at 418. Although the Clause gives Congress authority to "legislate on that vast mass of incidental powers which must be involved in the constitution," it does not license the exercise of any "great substantive and independent power[s]" beyond those specifically enumerated. Id., at 411, 421. Instead, the Clause is " 'merely a declaration, for the removal of all uncertainty, that the means of carrying into execution those [powers] otherwise granted are included in the grant.' " Kinsella v. United States ex rel. Singleton, 361 U.S. 234, 247, 80 S.Ct. 297, 4 L.Ed.2d 268 (1960) (quoting VI Writings of James Madison 383 (G. Hunt ed. 1906)).

As our jurisprudence under the Necessary and Proper Clause has developed, we have been very deferential to Congress's determination that a regulation is "necessary." We have thus upheld laws that are " 'convenient, or useful' or 'conducive' to the authority's 'beneficial exercise.' " Comstock, 560 U.S., at ——, 130 S.Ct., at 1965 (quoting McCulloch, supra, at 413, 418). But we have also carried out our responsibility to declare unconstitutional those laws that undermine the structure of government established by the Constitution. Such laws, which are not "consist[ent] with the letter and spirit of the constitution," McCulloch, supra, at 421, are not "proper [means] for carrying into Execution" Congress's enumerated powers. Rather, they are, "in the words of The Federalist, 'merely acts of usurpation' which 'deserve to be treated as such.' " Printz v. United States, 521 U.S. 898, 924, 117 S.Ct. 2365, 138 L.Ed.2d 914 (1997) (alterations omitted) (quoting

The Federalist No. 33, at 204 (A. Hamilton)); see also New York, 505 U.S., at 177, 112 S.Ct. 2408; Comstock, supra, at ——, 130 S.Ct., at 1967–1968 (KENNEDY, J., concurring in judgment) ("It is of fundamental importance to consider whether essential attributes of state sovereignty are compromised by the assertion of federal power under the Necessary and Proper Clause ...").

Applying these principles, the individual mandate cannot be sustained under the Necessary and Proper Clause as an essential component of the insurance reforms. Each of our prior cases upholding laws under that Clause involved exercises of authority derivative of, and in service to, a granted power. For example, we have upheld provisions permitting continued confinement of those already in federal custody when they could not be safely released, Comstock, supra, at ——, 130 S.Ct., at 1954–1955; criminalizing bribes involving organizations receiving federal funds, Sabri v. United States, 541 U.S. 600, 602, 605, 124 S.Ct. 1941, 158 L.Ed.2d 891 (2004); and tolling state statutes of limitations while cases are pending in federal court, Jinks v. Richland County, 538 U.S. 456, 459, 462, 123 S.Ct. 1667, 155 L.Ed.2d 631 (2003). The individual mandate, by contrast, vests Congress with the extraordinary ability to create the necessary predicate to the exercise of an enumerated power.

This is in no way an authority that is "narrow in scope," Comstock, supra, at ——, 130 S.Ct., at 1964, or "incidental" to the exercise of the commerce power, McCulloch, supra, at 418. Rather, such a conception of the Necessary and Proper Clause would work a substantial expansion of federal authority. No longer would Congress be limited to regulating under the Commerce Clause those who by some preexisting activity bring themselves within the sphere of federal regulation. Instead, Congress could reach beyond the natural limit of its authority and draw within its regulatory scope those who otherwise would be outside of it. Even if the individual mandate is "necessary" to the Act's insurance reforms, such an expansion of federal power is not a "proper" means for making those reforms effective.

The Government relies primarily on our decision in Gonzales v. Raich. In Raich, we considered "comprehensive legislation to regulate the interstate market" in marijuana. 545 U.S., at 22, 125 S.Ct. 2195. Certain individuals sought an exemption from that regulation on the ground that they engaged in only intrastate possession and consumption. We denied any exemption, on the ground that marijuana is a fungible commodity, so that any marijuana could be readily diverted into the interstate market. Congress's attempt to regulate the interstate market for marijuana would therefore have been substantially undercut if it could not also regulate intrastate possession and consumption. Id., at 19, 125 S.Ct. 2195. Accordingly, we recognized that "Congress was acting well within its authority" under the Necessary and Proper Clause even though its "regulation ensnare[d] some purely intrastate activity." Id., at 22, 125 S.Ct. 2195; see also Perez, 402 U.S., at 154, 91 S.Ct. 1357. Raich thus did not involve the exercise of any "great substantive and independent power," McCulloch, supra, at 411, of the sort at issue here. Instead, it concerned only the constitutionality of "individual applications of a concededly valid statutory scheme." Raich, supra, at 23, 125 S.Ct. 2195 (emphasis added).

Just as the individual mandate cannot be sustained as a law regulating the substantial effects of the failure to purchase health insurance, neither can it be upheld as a "necessary and proper" component of the insurance reforms. The commerce power thus does not authorize the mandate. Accord, post, at 2644 – 2650 (joint opinion of SCALIA, KENNEDY, THOMAS, and ALITO, JJ., dissenting).

B

That is not the end of the matter. Because the Commerce Clause does not support the individual mandate, it is necessary to turn to the Government's second argument: that the mandate may be upheld as within Congress's enumerated power to "lay and collect Taxes." Art. I, § 8, cl. 1.

The Government's tax power argument asks us to view the statute differently than we did in considering its commerce power theory. In making its Commerce Clause argument, the Government defended the mandate as a regulation requiring individuals to purchase health insurance. The Government does not claim that the taxing power allows Congress to issue such a command. Instead, the Government asks us to read the mandate not as ordering individuals to buy insurance, but rather as imposing a tax on those who do not buy that product.

The text of a statute can sometimes have more than one possible meaning. To take a familiar example, a law that reads "no vehicles in the park" might, or might not, ban bicycles in the park. And it is well established that if a statute has two possible meanings, one of which violates the Constitution, courts should adopt the meaning that does not do so. Justice Story said that 180 years ago: "No court ought, unless the terms of an act rendered it unavoidable, to give a construction to it which should involve a violation, however unintentional, of the constitution." Parsons v. Bedford, 3 Pet. 433, 448–449, 7 L.Ed. 732 (1830). Justice Holmes made the same point a century later: "[T]he rule is settled that as between two possible interpretations of a statute, by one of which it would be unconstitutional and by the other valid, our plain duty is to adopt that which will save the Act." Blodgett v. Holden, 275 U.S. 142, 148, 48 S.Ct. 105, 72 L.Ed. 206 (1927) (concurring opinion).

The most straightforward reading of the mandate is that it commands individuals to purchase insurance. After all, it states that individuals "shall" maintain health insurance. 26 U.S.C. § 5000A(a). Congress thought it could enact such a command under the Commerce Clause, and the Government primarily defended the law on that basis. But, for the reasons explained above, the Commerce Clause does not give Congress that power. Under our precedent, it is therefore necessary to ask whether the Government's alternative reading of the statute— that it only imposes a tax on those without insurance—is a reasonable one.

Under the mandate, if an individual does not maintain health insurance, the only consequence is that he must make an additional payment to the IRS when he pays his taxes. See § 5000A(b). That, according to the Government, means the mandate can be regarded as establishing a condition—not owning health insurance—that triggers a tax—the required payment to the IRS. Under that theory, the mandate is not a legal command to buy insurance. Rather, it makes going without insurance just another thing the Government taxes, like buying gasoline or earning income. And if the mandate is in effect just a tax hike on certain taxpayers who do not have health insurance, it may be within Congress's constitutional power to tax.

The question is not whether that is the most natural interpretation of the mandate, but only whether it is a "fairly possible" one. Crowell v. Benson, 285 U.S. 22, 62, 52 S.Ct. 285, 76 L.Ed. 598 (1932). As we have explained, "every reasonable construction must be resorted to, in order to save a statute from unconstitutionality." Hooper v. California, 155 U.S. 648, 657, 15 S.Ct. 207, 39 L.Ed. 297 (1895). The Government asks us to interpret the mandate as imposing a tax, if it would otherwise violate the Constitution. Granting the Act the full measure of deference owed to federal statutes, it can be so read, for the reasons set forth below.

C

The exaction the Affordable Care Act imposes on those without health insurance looks like a tax in many respects. The "[s]hared responsibility payment," as the statute entitles it, is paid into the Treasury by "taxpayer[s]" when they file their tax returns. 26 U.S.C. § 5000A(b). It does not apply to individuals who do not pay federal income taxes because their household income is less than the filing threshold in the Internal Revenue Code. § 5000A(e)(2). For taxpayers who do owe the payment, its amount is determined by such familiar factors as taxable income, number of dependents, and joint filing status. §§ 5000A(b)(3), (c)(2), (c)(4). The requirement to pay is found in the Internal Revenue Code and enforced by the IRS, which—as we previously explained—must assess and collect it "in the same manner as taxes." Supra, at 2583 – 2584. This process yields the essential feature of any tax: it produces at least some revenue for the Government. United States v. Kahriger, 345 U.S. 22, 28, n. 4, 73 S.Ct. 510, 97 L.Ed. 754 (1953). Indeed, the payment is expected to raise about $4 billion per year by 2017. Congressional Budget Office, Payments of Penalties for Being Uninsured Under the Patient Protection and Affordable Care Act (Apr. 30, 2010), in Selected CBO Publications Related to Health Care Legislation, 2009–2010, p. 71 (rev. 2010).

It is of course true that the Act describes the payment as a "penalty," not a "tax." But while that label is fatal to the application of the Anti–Injunction Act, supra, at 2582 – 2583, it does not determine whether the payment may be viewed as an exercise of Congress's taxing power. It is up to Congress whether to apply the Anti–Injunction Act to any particular statute, so it makes sense to be guided by Congress's choice of label on that question. That choice does not, however, control whether an exaction is within Congress's constitutional power to tax.

Our precedent reflects this: In 1922, we decided two challenges to the "Child Labor Tax" on the same day. In the first, we held that a suit to enjoin collection of the so-called tax was barred by the Anti–Injunction Act.   George, 259 U.S., at 20, 42 S.Ct. 419. Congress knew that suits to obstruct taxes had to await payment under the Anti–Injunction Act; Congress called the child labor tax a tax; Congress therefore intended the Anti–Injunction Act to apply. In the second case, however, we held that the same exaction, although labeled a tax, was not in fact authorized by Congress's taxing power. Drexel Furniture, 259 U.S., at 38, 42 S.Ct. 449. That constitutional question was not controlled by Congress's choice of label.

We have similarly held that exactions not labeled taxes nonetheless were authorized by Congress's power to tax. In the License Tax Cases, for example, we held that federal licenses to sell liquor and lottery tickets—for which the licensee had to pay a fee—could be sustained as exercises of the taxing power. 5 Wall., at 471. And in New York v. United States we upheld as a tax a "surcharge" on out-of-state nuclear waste shipments, a portion of which was paid to the Federal Treasury. 505 U.S., at 171, 112 S.Ct. 2408. We thus ask whether the shared responsibility payment falls within Congress's taxing power, "[d]isregarding the designation of the exaction, and viewing its substance and application." United States v. Constantine, 296 U.S. 287, 294, 56 S.Ct. 223, 80 L.Ed. 233 (1935); cf. Quill Corp. v. North Dakota, 504 U.S. 298, 310, 112 S.Ct. 1904, 119 L.Ed.2d 91 (1992) ("[M]agic words or labels" should not "disable an otherwise constitutional levy" (internal quotation marks omitted)); Nelson v. Sears, Roebuck & Co., 312 U.S. 359, 363, 61 S.Ct. 586, 85 L.Ed. 888 (1941) ("In passing on the constitutionality of a tax law, we are concerned only with its practical operation, not its definition or the precise form of descriptive words which may be applied to it" (internal quotation marks omitted)); United States v. Sotelo, 436 U.S. 268, 275, 98 S.Ct. 1795, 56 L.Ed.2d 275 (1978) ("That the funds due are referred to as a 'penalty' ... does not alter their essential character as taxes").

Our cases confirm this functional approach. For example, in Drexel Furniture, we focused on three practical characteristics of the so-called tax on employing child laborers that convinced us the "tax" was actually a penalty. First, the tax imposed an exceedingly heavy burden—10 percent of a company's net income—on those who employed children, no matter how small their infraction. Second, it imposed that exaction only on those who knowingly employed underage laborers. Such scienter requirements are typical of punitive statutes, because Congress often wishes to punish only those who intentionally break the law. Third, this "tax" was enforced in part by the Department of Labor, an agency responsible for punishing violations of labor laws, not collecting revenue. 259 U.S., at 36–37, 42 S.Ct. 449; see also, e.g., Kurth Ranch, 511 U.S., at 780–782, 114 S.Ct. 1937 (considering, inter alia, the amount of the exaction, and the fact that it was imposed for violation of a separate criminal law); Constantine, supra, at 295, 56 S.Ct. 223 (same).

The same analysis here suggests that the shared responsibility payment may for constitutional purposes be considered a tax, not a penalty: First, for most Americans the amount due will be far less than the price of insurance, and, by statute, it can never be more. It may often be a reasonable financial decision to make the payment rather than purchase insurance, unlike the "prohibitory" financial punishment in Drexel Furniture. 259 U.S., at 37, 42 S.Ct. 449. Second, the individual mandate contains no scienter requirement. Third, the payment is collected solely by the IRS through the normal means of taxation—except that the Service is not allowed to use those means most suggestive of a punitive sanction, such as criminal prosecution. See § 5000A(g)(2). The reasons the Court in Drexel Furniture held that what was called a "tax" there was a penalty support the conclusion that what is called a "penalty" here may be viewed as a tax.

None of this is to say that the payment is not intended to affect individual conduct. Although the payment will raise considerable revenue, it is plainly designed to expand health insurance coverage. But taxes that seek to influence conduct are nothing new. Some of our earliest federal taxes sought to deter the purchase of imported manufactured goods in order to foster the growth of domestic industry. See W. Brownlee, Federal Taxation in America 22 (2d ed. 2004); cf. 2 J. Story, Commentaries on the Constitution of the United States § 962, p. 434 (1833) ("the taxing power is often, very often, applied for other purposes, than revenue"). Today, federal and state taxes can compose more than half the retail price of cigarettes, not just to raise more money, but to encourage people to quit smoking. And we have upheld such obviously regulatory measures as taxes on selling marijuana and sawed-off shotguns. See United States v. Sanchez, 340 U.S. 42, 44–45, 71 S.Ct. 108, 95 L.Ed. 47 (1950); Sonzinsky v. United States, 300 U.S. 506, 513, 57 S.Ct. 554, 81 L.Ed. 772 (1937). Indeed, "[e]very tax is in some measure regulatory. To some extent it interposes an economic impediment to the activity taxed as compared with others not taxed." Sonzinsky, supra, at 513, 57 S.Ct. 554. That § 5000A seeks to shape decisions about whether to buy health insurance does not mean that it cannot be a valid exercise of the taxing power.

In distinguishing penalties from taxes, this Court has explained that "if the concept of penalty means anything, it means punishment for an unlawful act or omission." United States v. Reorganized CF & I Fabricators of Utah, Inc., 518 U.S. 213, 224, 116 S.Ct. 2106, 135 L.Ed.2d 506 (1996); see also United States v. La Franca, 282 U.S. 568, 572, 51 S.Ct. 278, 75 L.Ed. 551 (1931) ("[A] penalty, as the word is here used, is an exaction imposed by statute as punishment for an unlawful act"). While the individual mandate clearly aims to induce the purchase of health insurance, it need not be read to declare that failing to do so is unlawful. Neither the Act nor any other law attaches negative legal consequences to not buying health insurance, beyond requiring a payment to the IRS. The Government agrees with that reading, confirming that if someone chooses to pay rather than obtain health insurance, they have fully complied with the law. Brief for United States 60–61; Tr. of Oral Arg. 49–50 (Mar. 26, 2012).

Indeed, it is estimated that four million people each year will choose to pay the IRS rather than buy insurance. See Congressional Budget Office, supra, at 71. We would expect Congress to be troubled by that prospect if such conduct were unlawful. That Congress apparently regards such extensive failure to comply with the mandate as tolerable suggests that Congress did not think it was creating four million outlaws. It suggests instead that the shared responsibility payment merely imposes a tax citizens may lawfully choose to pay in lieu of buying health insurance.

The plaintiffs contend that Congress's choice of language—stating that individuals "shall" obtain insurance or pay a "penalty"—requires reading § 5000A as punishing unlawful conduct, even if that interpretation would render the law unconstitutional. We have rejected a similar argument before. In New York v. United States we examined a statute providing that " '[e]ach State shall be responsible for providing ... for the disposal of ... low-level radioactive waste.'" 505 U.S., at 169, 112 S.Ct. 2408 (quoting 42 U.S.C. § 2021c(a)(1)(A)). A State that shipped its waste to another State was exposed to surcharges by the receiving State, a portion of which would be paid over to the Federal Government. And a State that did not adhere to the statutory scheme faced "[p]enalties for failure to comply," including increases in the surcharge. § 2021e(e)(2); New York, 505 U.S., at 152–153, 112 S.Ct. 2408. New York urged us to read the statute as a federal command that the state legislature enact legislation to dispose of its waste, which would have violated the Constitution. To avoid that outcome, we interpreted the statute to impose only "a series of incentives" for the State to take responsibility for its waste. We then sustained the charge paid to the Federal Government as an exercise of the taxing power. Id., at 169–174, 112 S.Ct. 2408. We see no insurmountable obstacle to a similar approach here.

The joint dissenters argue that we cannot uphold § 5000A as a tax because Congress did not "frame" it as such. Post, at 2650 – 2651. In effect, they contend that even if the Constitution permits Congress to do exactly what we interpret this statute to do, the law must be struck down because Congress used the wrong labels. An example may help illustrate why labels should not control here. Suppose Congress enacted a statute providing that every taxpayer who owns a house without energy efficient windows must pay $50 to the IRS. The amount due is adjusted based on factors such as taxable income and joint filing status, and is paid along with the taxpayer's income tax return. Those whose income is below the filing threshold need not pay. The required payment is not called a "tax," a "penalty," or anything else. No one would doubt that this law imposed a tax, and was within Congress's power to tax. That conclusion should not change simply because Congress used the word "penalty" to describe the payment. Interpreting such a law to be a tax would hardly "[i]mpos[e] a tax through judicial legislation." Post, at 2655. Rather, it would give practical effect to the Legislature's enactment.

Our precedent demonstrates that Congress had the power to impose the exaction in § 5000A under the taxing power, and that § 5000A need not be read to do more than impose a tax. That is sufficient to sustain it. The "question of the constitutionality of action taken by Congress does not depend on recitals of the power which it undertakes to exercise." Woods v. Cloyd W. Miller Co., 333 U.S. 138, 144, 68 S.Ct. 421, 92 L.Ed. 596 (1948).

Even if the taxing power enables Congress to impose a tax on not obtaining health insurance, any tax must still comply with other requirements in the Constitution. Plaintiffs argue that the shared responsibility payment does not do so, citing Article I, § 9, clause 4. That clause provides: "No Capitation, or other direct, Tax shall be laid, unless in Proportion to the Census or Enumeration herein before directed to be taken." This requirement means that any "direct Tax" must be apportioned so that each State pays in proportion to its population. According to the plaintiffs, if the individual mandate imposes a tax, it is a direct tax, and it is unconstitutional because Congress made no effort to apportion it among the States.

Even when the Direct Tax Clause was written it was unclear what else, other than a capitation (also known as a "head tax" or a "poll tax"), might be a direct tax. See Springer v. United States, 102 U.S. 586, 596–598, 26 L.Ed. 253 (1881). Soon after the framing, Congress passed a tax on ownership of carriages, over James Madison's objection that it was an unapportioned direct tax. Id., at 597. This Court upheld the tax, in part reasoning that apportioning such a tax would make little sense, because it would have required taxing carriage owners at dramatically different rates depending on how many carriages were in their home State. See Hylton v. United States, 3 Dall. 171, 174, 1 L.Ed. 556 (1796) (opinion of Chase, J.). The Court was unanimous, and those Justices who wrote opinions either directly asserted or strongly suggested that only two forms of taxation were direct: capitations and land taxes. See id., at 175; id., at 177 (opinion of Paterson, J.); id., at 183 (opinion of Iredell, J.).

That narrow view of what a direct tax might be persisted for a century. In 1880, for example, we explained that "direct taxes, within the meaning of the Constitution, are only capitation taxes, as expressed in that instrument, and taxes on real estate." Springer, supra, at 602. In 1895, we expanded our interpretation to include taxes on personal property and income from personal property, in the course of striking down aspects of the federal income tax. Pollock v. Farmers' Loan & Trust Co., 158 U.S. 601, 618, 15 S.Ct. 912, 39 L.Ed. 1108 (1895). That result was overturned by the Sixteenth Amendment, although we continued to consider taxes on personal property to be direct taxes. See Eisner v. Macomber, 252 U.S. 189, 218–219, 40 S.Ct. 189, 64 L.Ed. 521 (1920).

A tax on going without health insurance does not fall within any recognized category of direct tax. It is not a capitation. Capitations are taxes paid by every person, "without regard to property, profession, or any other circumstance." Hylton, supra, at 175 (opinion of Chase, J.) (emphasis altered). The whole point of the shared responsibility payment is that it is triggered by specific circumstances—earning a certain amount of income but not obtaining health insurance. The payment is also plainly not a tax on the ownership of land or personal property. The shared responsibility payment is thus not a direct tax that must be apportioned among the several States.

There may, however, be a more fundamental objection to a tax on those who lack health insurance. Even if only a tax, the payment under § 5000A(b) remains a burden that the Federal Government imposes for an omission, not an act. If it is troubling to interpret the Commerce Clause as authorizing Congress to regulate those who abstain from commerce, perhaps it should be similarly troubling to permit Congress to impose a tax for not doing something.

Three considerations allay this concern. First, and most importantly, it is abundantly clear the Constitution does not guarantee that individuals may avoid taxation through inactivity. A capitation, after all, is a tax that everyone must pay simply for existing, and capitations are expressly contemplated by the Constitution. The Court today holds that our Constitution protects us from federal regulation under the Commerce Clause so long as we abstain from the regulated activity. But from its creation, the Constitution has made no such promise with respect to taxes. See Letter from Benjamin Franklin to M. Le Roy (Nov. 13, 1789) ("Our new Constitution is now established ... but in this world nothing can be said to be certain, except death and taxes").

Whether the mandate can be upheld under the Commerce Clause is a question about the scope of federal authority. Its answer depends on whether Congress can exercise what all acknowledge to be the novel course of directing individuals to purchase insurance. Congress's use of the Taxing Clause to encourage buying something is, by contrast, not new. Tax incentives already promote, for example, purchasing homes and professional educations. See 26 U.S.C. §§ 163(h), 25A. Sustaining the mandate as a tax depends only on whether Congress has properly exercised its taxing power to encourage purchasing health insurance, not whether it can. Upholding the individual mandate under the Taxing Clause thus does not recognize any new federal power. It determines that Congress has used an existing one.

Second, Congress's ability to use its taxing power to influence conduct is not without limits. A few of our cases policed these limits aggressively, invalidating punitive exactions obviously designed to regulate behavior otherwise regarded at the time as beyond federal authority. See, e.g., United States v. Butler, 297 U.S. 1, 56 S.Ct. 312, 80 L.Ed. 477 (1936); Drexel Furniture, 259 U.S. 20, 42 S.Ct. 449, 66 L.Ed. 817. More often and more recently we have declined to closely examine the regulatory motive or effect of revenue-raising measures. See Kahriger, 345 U.S., at 27–31, 73 S.Ct. 510 (collecting cases). We have nonetheless maintained that " 'there comes a time in the extension of the penalizing features of the so-called tax when it loses its character as such and becomes a mere penalty with the characteristics of regulation and punishment.' " Kurth Ranch, 511 U.S., at 779, 114 S.Ct. 1937 (quoting Drexel Furniture, supra, at 38, 42 S.Ct. 449).

We have already explained that the shared responsibility payment's practical characteristics pass muster as a tax under our narrowest interpretations of the taxing power. Supra, at 2595 – 2596. Because the tax at hand is within even those strict limits, we need not here decide the precise point at which an exaction becomes so punitive that the taxing power does not authorize it. It remains true, however, that the " 'power to tax is not the power to destroy while this Court sits.' " Oklahoma Tax Comm'n v. Texas Co., 336 U.S. 342, 364, 69 S.Ct. 561, 93 L.Ed. 721 (1949) (quoting Panhandle Oil Co. v. Mississippi ex rel. Knox, 277 U.S. 218, 223, 48 S.Ct. 451, 72 L.Ed. 857 (1928) (Holmes, J., dissenting)).

Third, although the breadth of Congress's power to tax is greater than its power to regulate commerce, the taxing power does not give Congress the same degree of control over individual behavior. Once we recognize that Congress may regulate a particular decision under the Commerce Clause, the Federal Government can bring its full weight to bear. Congress may simply command individuals to do as it directs. An individual who disobeys may be subjected to criminal sanctions. Those sanctions can include not only fines and imprisonment, but all the attendant consequences of being branded a criminal: deprivation of otherwise protected civil rights, such as the right to bear arms or vote in elections; loss of employment opportunities; social stigma; and severe disabilities in other controversies, such as custody or immigration disputes.

By contrast, Congress's authority under the taxing power is limited to requiring an individual to pay money into the Federal Treasury, no more. If a tax is properly paid, the Government has no power to compel or punish individuals subject to it. We do not make light of the severe burden that taxation—especially taxation motivated by a regulatory purpose—can impose. But imposition of a tax nonetheless leaves an individual with a lawful choice to do or not do a certain act, so long as he is willing to pay a tax levied on that choice.

The Affordable Care Act's requirement that certain individuals pay a financial penalty for not obtaining health insurance may reasonably be characterized as a tax. Because the Constitution permits such a tax, it is not our role to forbid it, or to pass upon its wisdom or fairness. . . .

It is so ordered....

ABOUT THE AUTHOR

Einer Elhauge is the Petrie Professor of Law at Harvard Law School and the Founding Director of the Petrie-Flom Center in Health Law Policy, Biotechnology and Bioethics. For his website and publications, see
http://www.law.harvard.edu/faculty/elhauge/

He served as Chairman of the Antitrust Advisory Committee to the Obama Campaign. He teaches a gamut of courses ranging from Antitrust, Contracts, Corporations, Legislation, and Health Care Law. Before coming to Harvard, he was a Professor of Law at the University of California at Berkeley, and clerked for Judge Norris on the 9th Circuit and Justice Brennan on the Supreme Court. He received both his A.B. and his J.D. from Harvard, graduating first in his law school class.

He is an author of numerous pieces on range of topics even broader than he teaches, including antitrust (monopolization, predatory pricing, tying, bundled discounts, loyalty discounts, disgorgement, petitioning and state action immunity, the Google Books Settlement, and the Harvard v. Chicago schools of antitrust), public law (statutory interpretation, legislative term limits, the 2000 Presidential election, the ObamaCare mandate, and the implications of interest group theory for judicial review), corporate law (social responsibility and sale of control doctrine), patent law (patent holdup and royalty stacking), the legal profession (the value of litigation and counseling advice), and health law policy (healthcare fragmentation, medical technology assessment, how to make health law a coherent legal field, and how to devise a morally just and cost effective medical system). His most recent books include: "Research Handbook on the Economics of Antitrust Law (Edward Elgar Publishing Ltd. 2012)"; "The Fragmentation of U.S. Health Care: Causes and Solutions" (Oxford University Press 2010); "Statutory Default Rules" (Harvard University Press 2008); "U.S. Antitrust Law and Economics (Foundation Press 2011)"; and "Global Competition Law and Economics" (Hart Publishing 2011). Currently he is writing books about Contract Theory, Health Law Policy, and Re-engineering Human Biology, as well as working on articles on sundry other topics.

He signed on to an amicus brief of health law professors supporting the constitutionality of Obamacare, which was limited to explaining certain technical features of health law and did not get into the issues discussed in this book.